ONE SMALL FOOTPRINT

Molly Weir was born in Glasgow and spent her early years there. She started writing at school and had her first article accepted by the *Glasgow Evening Times*, at the age of fifteen. From then on she had freelanced 'as the mood takes her' for newspapers and magazines. In between engagements for TV, radio, films and the stage, she has written radio scripts for 'Woman's Hour', 'Home This Afternoon' and 'Children's Hour'.

Molly Weir

ONE SMALL FOOTPRINT

ARROW BOOKS

Arrow Books Limited
17–21 Conway Street, London W1P 5HL

An imprint of the Hutchinson Publishing Group

London Melbourne Sydney Auckland
Johannesburg and agencies
throughout the world

First published by Hutchinson 1980
Arrow edition 1982
© Molly Weir 1980

Made and printed in Great Britain
by The Anchor Press Ltd
Tiptree, Essex

ISBN 0 09 928040 X

FOR BEN

Who taught me one great truth:
Activity breeds Activity.

Blessed is he who has found his work.
Let him ask no other blessing.

CARLYLE

Putting off the easy thing makes it hard.
Putting off the hard thing makes it impossible.

GEORGE HORACE LATIMER

The indulgence of ease is fatal to excellence.

ANON

1

In my childhood, every Hogmanay followed the same traditional pattern. The last speck of dust was swept from the household gods, the ashes from the fireplace were emptied, and the best lace-trimmed cloth was put on the wee table in the front room. Then my mother would bring out the ginger wine, the whisky, the cake and the shortbread, which were set carefully on the snowy cloth. For she, and Grannie, and every other Scot throughout the length and breadth of the land held firm to the old beliefs that the way you started the year set the pattern for the twelve months which lay ahead.

So with plenty of friends to toast the New Year, having prudently made sure that the darkest-haired male was pushed in first to be the 'first foot', friendship and fellowship would be certain to follow. If we were all in good health, that was a most encouraging omen. And if the wage earner was in a good job, prosperity was practically guaranteed – for another year at least.

Brought up to have complete trust in this tradition, I always felt that the best possible start to the year was to be working. Paradoxically though, the fact that I was working meant that I couldn't enjoy the final touch to the Scottish Ne'erday celebrations, and that was a holiday on New Year's day.

For, as the only Scot in the cast of Britain's favourite radio family, *Life with the Lyons*, I was the loser every year when the arguments began as to whether we ought to work over Christmas or New Year.

I'd been playing the part of Aggie the cook-cum-house-keeper for five years and more by this time, and I dearly loved the Lyons. I could hardly remember a time when they hadn't filled most of my working life, but I could have throttled them because they wouldn't make it turn and turn about to have Christmas off one year, and New Year the next. Like a mutinous bairn, I'd practically wail, 'But it's not *fair*. You should celebrate the Scottish traditions one year and the English the next.'

'Too bad, honey,' Ben would grin, 'you're outnumbered. You're the only heathen who celebrates – what is it you call it? Hogmanay – so you just gotta accept the majority vote. We work Hogmanay and New Year's day.'

My mother was on my side. 'Can ye no' juist tell Ben that naebody works up here on New Year's day? Efter a', everybody knows it's a holiday. I'm shair if ye tellt Bebe she'd let you off.'

I shook my head. Och, it was my own choice after all that I was working in London. How could I expect the English or the Americans to change their customs just to suit me? Aye, and if Grannie and my mother were right I'd be daft to try to alter the pattern of the last five years, when I'd worked every New Year's day; and each of those years had been filled with enough radio, TV and film work to have convinced any doubting Thomas that there was indeed truth in the Scottish belief that a busy start to the year set the feet on the road to prosperity and success.

By the end of that year, 1956, when I looked back at the amazing variety of shows and experiences I'd enjoyed, and the challenges I'd had to face, I was very glad I'd clung to the old superstitious beliefs, and resisted the temptation of my mother's advice to be asked 'to be let off' on New Year's day.

An expression of my mother's which greatly intrigued me as a wee girl was the one she used with a deep sigh after an intent study of the births, deaths and marriages in *The Glasgow Times*, a newspaper she greatly favoured. Shaking her head sadly, she would click her tongue with a vexed 't't't' sound, and murmur, 'My, and him in the prime of life too.'

8

What was the prime of life? I wondered.

And why was it so sad to be taken in one's prime?

When my mother tried to explain, I couldn't see why she was so moved. It seemed to me rather splendid to be whipped off before 'age could wither or the years condemn', and I soulfully quoted the rest of the passage which I'd heard every year at Armistice services, 'At the going down of the sun and in the morning, we will remember them.' I was a great one for poetic language!

'Aye,' said my mother tartly, 'ye'll maybe change yer tune when yer in yer prime yersel'.'

Glancing back at the end of 1956 my mother's words came back to me. Could this be my prime? I wondered. If it was, my mother was right. I *had* changed my tune. I was delighted I was still here to enjoy it all, and not be a line in that dreaded column, to be sighed over by some unknown reader who would shake a mournful head and murmur, 'And in her prime too.'

The words which now stirred me were, 'Today is the first day of the rest of your life. Don't waste it!'

The first exciting thing that happened in that action-packed year was on 7 January when our very first car arrived. Brand new from the showrooms. As far as I was concerned it was merely an ornament, for I couldn't drive. It was a mysterious beast which had to be conquered, and I was determined in the fullness of time I'd manage it.

What inspired this purchase was the arrival of commercial television. I hadn't been particularly concerned about this, and was astonished to be asked to do my very first advertisement. Everybody was dying to get into this lucrative side of show business, and I, who hadn't moved a muscle in that direction, landed one of the very first jobs in advertising. To the amusement of friends and neighbours, I'd been asked to promote the sale of the latest Morris car. Everybody who knew me was aware that I couldn't even ride a bicycle, much less drive a car. Nevertheless, I was to be filmed sitting at the wheel of a lovely new pale grey Morris, looking suitably thrilled with my purchase as I was about to drive myself into town in my new car.

I'd never even sat in the driving seat of a car, and it felt very smart to be sitting there with my hands on the wheel, dressed in my best Jacqmar suit and matching hat, checking that the road ahead was clear.

As soon as they'd filmed that part of the advertisement I slipped out, and a real driver changed into my clothes. I commanded her not to zip up the skirt in case she'd bust it. It was my best suit after all, and I wasn't so carried away with all this glamour that I wanted it ruined by somebody who clearly had broader hips than mine!

She wore a pageboy style wig, a marvellous imitation of my hairstyle, and when she'd popped my hat on top, and sat with her back to the camera, and placed her hands on the wheel, ready to do a tricky bit of parking into the tightest possible space, you'd have sworn it was me.

When this bit of trickery was completed, she nipped out, and we changed clothes again, and back into the car I went, hands on the wheel as before, smiling triumphantly into the camera, obviously delighted with myself for having acquired such a manoeuvrable vehicle.

It was so well filmed and cut that when I saw the finished advertisement, I could hardly believe I hadn't done the whole thing myself. Our local bobby knew I hadn't though! *He* had cause in later months to shake his head sadly over my abominable parking! 'Aye,' he'd say. '*You* never parked yon Morris, that's for sure!'

But all that was to come.

This enjoyable experience of pretending I had a car was so persuasive that I decided, with Sandy's enthusiastic approval, to buy a Morris for ourselves.

I was so naive that I never even thought of asking for a discount, although I'd advertised the thing for them. And of course if ye dinna ask, ye dinna get! I paid the full retail price, and what maddened me was that nobody would believe me! Those with a more sophisticated turn of mind said to me, 'But to be seen driving that car after advertising it was personal endorsement. You *must* have had a discount.'

I hadn't.

I didn't know about such things, but I could see disbelief in the eyes of the worldly ones, and I stopped protesting and just let them think what they liked.

The one advantage I did receive though, was to be pushed to the top of the queue to take delivery of a Clarendon grey model, for the demand was tremendous, and there was a long waiting list. The advert had proved its worth all right.

Now on the 7 January 1956 it stood in the drive. Our car!

Sandy was going to take driving lessons first, and when *he* passed, I would learn. Knowing my disastrous lack of skill with a pushbike, he was at first stunned that I would even attempt driving lessons. 'You'll never drive a car,' he said. 'I'd never know a minute's peace.'

It was my turn to be outraged.

'I'm not going to have that car sitting in the garage while you're at the office,' I said, 'and besides, I want to be able to drive my mother farther afield when we have her down for the summer. I'm sure she's fed up only getting as far as Pinner village and Ruislip. And she's getting a wee bit beyond walks involving miles of leg-work.'

When the time came for my driving lessons, Sandy having successfully passed his test, I was taught by an ex-police driver recommended to us by a girl in the film studios. She felt it would need someone of his stamina to handle a mettlesome creature like myself!

Long afterwards he told me that when he came to write his memoirs, I'd have a chapter all to myself. He told me he'd never come across anyone so fast and frightening in her reactions. Nor had he ever come across a female who could follow a drawing, and understand what she was looking at. This came about because I simply couldn't fathom what he was trying to tell me about a three-point turning.

'Draw it for me,' I said, handing him a piece of paper and a pen, items I always carry in my bag in case inspiration strikes!

'How will that help?' he'd asked. 'You won't be able to follow it.'

'Just draw it,' I said. 'I'll follow it.'

He drew the wheels. Then another set of wheels, showing what happened when the steering was altered. He then drew another set of wheels, with little arrows indicating what was happening. I looked at it intently, asked a question or two, took the wheel and did a perfect three-point turn.

He stared at me, shaking his head in disbelief. 'Well, you're the first woman I've met who can read a drawing,' he said at last.

'Of course,' I said. 'Don't you realize I am used to reading scripts, and seeing plans of sets for films and TV? Drawings are far easier for me than technical explanations of the mechanics.'

But it took two tests to give me a 'pass'. Again, the examiner was shaken by my speedy reactions. He was not going to tell me why I'd failed, but I made him. My eyes brimming with tears, I exclaimed with passionate drama that my mother was coming down on holiday, that I'd bought the car principally to give her an easier time, and that I just *had* to know what to polish if I were to be ready to drive her around while she was with us.

'Slow down,' he'd said, avoiding my tear-stained gaze. 'Slow down, and let me *see* you checking other traffic, and getting ready to move out. Don't do everything at such lightning speed.'

I was amazed. Could I have failed for simply being myself?

'But I do everything quickly,' I said. 'I talk quickly. I walk quickly. I move quickly. It's natural for me to do everything at a fast pace.'

'Not in a car it's not,' he said with a little asperity in his tone, 'not if you want to pass a test that is. Another month won't harm you at all, and it will certainly give you more experience on the roads.'

And that was that.

I could have throttled him.

I had to go through all that performance again. But I took note of his advice, and I passed at my second attempt.

Hallelujah!

My mother's reaction when she saw me at the wheel for the first time was quite hilarious. She wasn't in the least surprised. She assumed I could do anything, and couldn't even begin to guess the blood, sweat, toil and tears which had accompanied those early driving lessons. To her the great achievement was in being able to *buy* a car. Driving skill came with the receipt, she thought. It wasn't something which had to be *learned*, and even if it was, 'Oor Molly could manage onything.'

That 7 January was truly a red-letter-day. For not only did our car arrive on that date, but I'd been booked to appear that night in the one and only night club I was ever to enter. A commercial television company televised a live show each week from this famous Bond Street nightspot, where Geoff Love was resident band conductor, and various show business personalities were interviewed as they sat dining at the little tables.

For this exciting occasion I bought a strapless evening dress, and for underneath I bought a swooningly sophisticated strapless corset so that nothing would mar the line of the dress. No straps to be poked out of sight. No bumps anywhere of unsuitable undies. I'd never worn a corset in my life, nor had I required the services of Sandy for the purpose of hooking me up, and he could hardly get hooks and eyes together for laughing. It was a first for him too! He said it was like playing in a French farce, with me gasping for breath as I was encased in this straitjacket.

The whole performance had to come to a halt when I burst into unladylike laughter as I remembered my old school chum and the school party which saw the end of our schooldays. She had called to collect me, wearing what we called 'stiff stays' to control her generous figure, and my brother Tommy made a drawing of her sitting on the edge of her chair, like a poker, unable to bend or to move.*

Best Foot Forward

Sandy on this occasion was part of the 'act', for we were supposed to be casually dining until interrupted by the interviewer, and once he'd been assured that the camera wouldn't go near him, was fairly looking forward to a first-class dinner. This club was famous for its food, as well as its company. I knew I'd be scared to eat a bite, being quite sure that the minute I put a piece of steak into my mouth, the TV chap would pounce on me, and I'd be caught talking with my mouth full. Or worse, choking if I attempted to eat during the chit-chat.

When we reached the club, I found to my delight that the others 'on the bill' were real superstars whom I'd not met before. Imagine my pleasure to find myself sitting beside Viera, the lovely international singing star, when I went into the makeshift dressing room where we were to be made up for the TV cameras and lighting. We all knew her from our TV screens. She was one of the early TV charmers, with a mellow pure singing tone which would have enchanted the birds from the trees. She sang in several languages, and she accompanied herself on the guitar with a true sense of music which made her a great favourite everywhere and appealed to all tastes.

I simply couldn't believe that she knew me. Somehow, although I had by this time done quite a lot on television, I had never imagined other performers would either look at me or know me. Particularly anyone of Viera's reputation. It gave me a new twinge of terror to think of such experts sitting in judgment every time I appeared on their screens, and I knew that I'd be aware of this from now on.

Dora Bryan, in a beautiful lace dress, was with her cricketer husband. She had me giggling with genuine amusement when she replied, in answer to somebody who asked her why she worked so hard. 'Well, it's the money, isn't it?' in those unmistakable Lancashire tones.

The fourth member of our little cast was the ballerina, Markova. She arrived late, when we were already seated at our various tables, surrounded by the club's patrons who were all eating and drinking merrily, not a care in the world.

Unlike us, who had a show to think about. Markova looked stunningly beautiful. She wore a very dark mink coat, over a black lace dress, and her face was so pale it was almost luminous in that lighting. Her black hair shone, and altogether she appeared romantic, exquisite, and every inch what one would expect of a ballerina of world renown.

Gosh, I felt very small fry in this setting.

However, I consoled myself that I wasn't there for my glamour, but for my comedy. Comedy! What comedy? I never felt less like a comedienne when I looked across at Dora Bryan serenely tucking into her lovely food, and was only conscious of that ghastly corset strangling me as I attempted to take deep breaths to calm my twittering butterflies!

But I did, after all manage to get a few laughs with my story of the car advertisement and of being my own best customer. And they were amused to be told the car had arrived that very morning. Then followed a few anecdotes from *Life with the Lyons* before the spotlight swept off me and on to Markova, and I was able to enjoy my dinner, now half cold.

Every time I see Geoff Love, who, happily, is still conducting and still working on television as I write, I am reminded of that unusual evening, the first time I was interviewed in a night club as a 'star' (ahem!), and the first time I was half asphyxiated in a strapless corset. It was a great relief when that fashion came to an end!

Whether or not it was the sight of me behind the wheel of the Morris in the TV advert which prompted them, I don't know, but the next invitation came from the organizers of a big charity ball. They wished me to judge the fancy dress parade and present the prizes, with Stirling Moss, then at the height of his fame as a racing driver. I agreed, for not only were we very curious and excited by the prospect of meeting Stirling Moss, but at that time I didn't know how to say 'no', or to protect my free time.

The ball was being held right at the other side of Middlesex, over an hour's drive from Pinner, even in good conditions, and the night it took place was one of thick suffocating fog. If we'd known more about the dangers of driving in fog, we'd not have put a foot outside the house, but innocents that we were, we meekly entered the car which had been sent to pick us up. Anyway, I'd given my word to be there, and I couldn't break it.

It was only by the grace of God that we reached Enfield unscathed over two hours later. We'd been driven up on the pavements, we were over on the wrong side of the road; we were up one-way streets in the wrong direction, down cul-de-sacs, in short we'd given a fair demonstration of being on a suicide mission.

I was shivering in my midnight blue velvet evening gown, and an icy perspiration gave signs that I was in the early stages of what later turned out to be one of my famous pulverizing doses of flu. At the time I'd thought it was merely the outward signs of the terror of the journey!

Stirling Moss made a breath-taking entrance riding a miniature car, which whizzed round the floor like a fire-cracker, and then he joined us for a soft drink. Rather surprisingly, his manager was with him. I didn't know then that stars were frequently accompanied either by their managers or their agents, who made sure the interests of their clients weren't threatened in any way. And also to make sure they weren't unduly pestered, or pressurized into making impossible promises. All awkward decisions could be passed to them, and no bones broken! Very handy.

The quality about Stirling Moss which most impressed me was his fantastic concentration. He had asked me to dance, and we found when we got on to the floor that it was an elimination dance, where everyone had to follow shouted instructions with instant obedience.

'Stand absolutely still,' came one command in the middle of a quick-step. We froze. Keeping my head quite still, I slid my eyes to the corners to see how many contestants were still in the game. Stirling's hand on my arm tightened in a grip of iron. 'Eyes still,' he breathed.

When the dance resumed, he said to me severely, 'We

ought to have been disqualified, because you moved your eyes!'

No wonder that chap won so many races. I had never dreamt for a moment that stillness extended to the eyeballs!

The next shouted instruction eliminated us as I wasn't wearing a petticoat, so I was spared the shame of confessing I'd broken the rules, had we gone on to be declared prize winners!

It was a very good lesson though, in the interpretation of a command, and a first-class demonstration of Moss's lightning responses. Mark you, *he* had tightened his hand on my arm, so he'd transgressed too!

After that, I seemed destined to be asked to everything connected with cars, and another charity ball found me with Mike Hawthorn (later to be tragically killed during an ordinary everyday drive from his home), and the talented Sheila Van Damm. I found the racing crowd stimulating, lively company, with a bubbling sense of fun behind their dedication, as though they were consciously living every moment of their lives. Petula Clark and I drew the prizes at that particular ball, and I felt that nowadays I was a member of a very exclusive club, where all invitations tended to find me rubbing shoulders with the top people from sport and entertainment.

It was no surprise, therefore, to be asked to take part in a Bacon Competition, of all things, at the Café Royal. Nor did I bat an eyelid at finding myself shadowed by Nancy Spain as I went round the various 'cuts' of the pig which we had to name and identify. She was a brilliant newspaper columnist and a fine speaker, a panellist and a broadcaster, and was so sought after for interviews that the whole country at that time knew she'd been educated at the top school for young ladies, Roedean. She was also a descendant of the great Mrs Beeton of the legendary cookery book.

As she peeked over my shoulder, I sent her into shouts of laughter by shielding my answers on the form and saying to her, 'Away ye go, Nancy Spain, nane o' yer cheatin' Roedean tricks here!' The mere idea that she could have anything to 'crib' from me was a joke we both shared, and for me it was fun to be able to use natural Glasgow humour and find a ready response in one whose background was a thousand miles from mine.

At the end of the evening, I'd won a gorgeous gammon, while Nancy was among the 'also-rans', and we ribbed her and told her that her famous ancestor would have been black affrontit to see her so far down the lists in the food-guessing stakes!

It was that sort of party, with everybody full of light-hearted teasing, and at the end Sam Heppner sat down at the piano and played song after song from Cole Porter, Gershwin, Irving Berlin, and Rodgers and Hart. We all joined in the choruses round the piano, with Stinker Murdoch and Carole Carr providing a touch of class singing the verses. Although she had a voice like a corncrake and couldn't hold a tune, I was fascinated to discover that Nancy Spain had the same facility with words as Denis Norden, and knew the words of every song played or sung. It was a dazzling display of memory, and if this facility awed me, it was nothing to Sandy's reaction. His own accuracy with the names of composers and movements of symphonies is quite impressive, but he can't remember more than half-a-dozen words of any song, so every time the name of Nancy Spain came up after that evening, he would gaze into the distance and recall the time of the singsong, when each and every melody found her with perfectly matching words.

She had the most marvellous head of hair, thick and wiry and strong, like a bass mat, and I could never resist patting it and bouncing my hand off its springiness when I passed her chair. Funnily enough, this hair also impressed Eric Linklater. I don't know if the Scots appreciate hair and teeth more than other people, but as soon as Eric Linklater knew that I was acquainted with Nancy, he said, 'Have you ever noticed her hair? Thick as a rug, and strong as wire.'

The whole country was plunged into sadness when the private plane in which she was travelling plummeted near the Aintree Race Course when it flew too low on the way to the afternoon's sport. All that vitality snuffed out in an instant. It was unbearable to contemplate.

She has been dead for many years now, but so strong was that challenging personality that I can see her face as clearly now, behind my closed lids, as on the evening when she leaned against the grand piano in the Café Royal and intoned the words of all the songs of all the popular composers of the day. An unforgettable spirit.

One of the most interesting TV jobs which now came my way was in a monthly series, for afternoon viewing, called *Room for Improvement*. I was to work with the top interior decorator of the day, John Siddeley (later to become Lord Kenilworth), and we were to busy ourselves solving the decorating and other problems of one room on each show. Viewers vied with one another to be chosen as the guinea pigs, and I loved the whole thing from first to last.

John of course was the expert, and he scoured the capital searching for just the right curtain materials, the carpets, the wallpapers and paint. There were then endless consultations as to how everything would be used to enhance the proportions of the rooms and to disguise awkward angles. Walls were sometimes knocked down, doors were re-hung, and a variety of alterations suggested.

The programme started each month with John and me in the background while the titles went up, and the tune *A Room with a View* introduced us. The whole thing was done live, and with our fingers crossed we'd launch ourselves into the programme, with 'before' and 'after' pictures of the room to dazzle the viewers. John explained the structural changes, while I concentrated on colour schemes, and asked the sort of questions I thought viewers would have asked had they been in the room with us.

Finally, the couple whose room had been selected for that month's experiment were brought on, and expressed their pleasure or otherwise in the transformation we'd wrought.

Monica Sims, now Controller of BBC Radio Four, was our producer. She always had a most original mind, and a keen eye for quality and performance, and she kept the whole thing lively and well-presented. The women viewers loved it, for they were, after all, getting John Siddeley's very expensive expertise for nothing. As for me, I adored the whole exercise. I was fairly intoxicated to be working with one of that rare breed whose path I never dreamed would ever have crossed mine, an interior decorator whose advice was sought by all the best people. When I thought back to my first adventure in decoration, when I stunned my mother and the neighbours by choosing pale blue and pale lemon for my first bedroom, at a time when all Glasgow decorated their homes in dirt-concealing browns, fawns and dark greens, I giggled with delight in my present job. When I'd changed the whole appearance of that tenement bedroom with my pastel tones, and carefully arranged drapes and fitments, I hadn't known that I was showing some awareness of 'interior decoration'. I did now, and I learned to my amazement that people were willing to pay 'braw saut', as my mother would have described it, to have experts do all the thinking and choosing for them.

What madness, I thought, to lose all the fun of working the miracle for themselves, and crowing over the transformation they alone had wrought. I didn't know that John Siddeley's clients were perfectly happy to concentrate on the talents which would allow them to earn the sort of cash which made his fees for doing the sort of work *he* was best at, seem like peanuts! An early lesson in getting the priorities right!

I always remember Barbara Lyon's surprise at a noticeable lack of rudimentary commonsense on the part of a maid she employed at that time, and when she complained of it to Ben, he turned and said with directness and simplicity, 'Honey, if she could think any other way, she wouldn't be earning a few pounds a week working for you. She'd be running her own business.'

Similarly, the rich left the work-a-day affairs to others whose job it was to attend to them, while they got on with the affairs best suited to their particular talents.

I learned all this and much more from that television programme, and in the end I'd absorbed so much, and had my natural love of colour and decoration so refined by rubbing shoulders with the best for all of six months, that I came to be regarded as a bit of an expert by friends and neighbours.

Selling flags round the doors, I'd be invited in and asked for my opinion on carpets, curtains and kitchens. Friends who acquired new houses sought my advice on colour schemes and equipment. And yet the one person who resisted my salesmanship and taste was Sandy! Truly a prophet is not without honour, save in her own country! I nearly had to go down on my bended knees to persuade him that the time had come to move the dark blue 'adapted' lounge carpet from our bedroom and change it for a pale cream which wouldn't show bed lint or talcum. He was horrified when I mentioned this change, and argued with some heat that I must be out of my mind, and that such a light carpet would show every mark. Needless to say, when eventually I had my way and the lovely top-of-the-milk shade of carpet stretched from wall to wall of our bedroom, he was so delighted at its continuously clean look that he believed he'd thought the whole thing out for himself, and now tells everyone that dark carpets are no use in bedrooms, for of course they show up all the fluff and powder! Like Brer Rabbit, I just lay low and say nothing. Well, most of the time I do!

Meantime Bebe and Ben were busy on the scripts for the next TV shows we'd been booked to do for the BBC on a six months' contract, and I was filling in the odd free days opening exhibitions and judging various contests. It's quite astonishing how often one's opinion is considered to be of value when one becomes a 'name' in the world of entertainment. It's very tempting to give instant decisions on every subject under the sun, and very valuable to have a husband, a mother, and friends and neighbours who see to it that you keep both feet soberly on the ground by treating you as the ordinary human being that you are.

During this 'marking time' period, Barbara Lyon had seized the opportunity to display her singing talent in a TV series called *Dreamtime with Barbara*. She'd inherited something of her mother's fine singing voice, and had something too of the style of Judy Garland. This, plus her own strikingly good looks made the show extremely successful. It's not too easy to be a member of a famous family and to try to branch out on your own, for comparisons are inevitable, and expectations much higher than if you were Suzy Snooks from next door. But Barbara proved she had her own appeal, and the viewing public found her little show very likeable and well worth watching. It was a most attractive début, and we were all very happy for her.

The producer of the show was Russell Turner, and he decided to carry *Dreamtime with Barbara* over into his private life by asking her to marry him!

Oh the excitement! When the announcement was made, we were again back on the air with our radio show, and our rehearsals at the Paris on the following day were interrupted by a veritable army of newsmen and photographers. We'd none of us, outside the family, seen Russell till that day and with typical Lyon flair he'd been written into the show for the following week. He was smallish, slight, and very dark. Nice looking and on the quiet side. I wondered if perhaps he wasn't too much of the average ordinary nice chap for Barbara, who had a strong personality, and in my opinion needed a pretty dominant male to strike a balance.

It was no part of my duty to voice any misgivings, for not only could I have been quite wrong but I'd be risking a black eye – or worse! So I stifled my inner qualms, and joined in the general congratulations, and posed with them and with the family for photographs for the press.

The next few months found me haring round the shops with Barbara, choosing linen, household goods, and dizzily expensive items for her trousseau. What bliss shopping for somebody else's wedding, and not having to look at every shilling twice! Barbara found to her amazement during those shopping expeditions, that she was now far more interested in buying things for the home than in choosing clothes for herself. I was the one who was drooling over suits and furs, while she weighed the advantages of this pan or that casserole against the practicalities of pressure cookers and the latest in ovenware. What a change was there, my friends! And from the first, she was determined to have a roof garden where she could grow as many shrubs and flowers as possible in her little corner of the asphalt jungle.

The house they bought was in an 'up-market' area of Notting Hill and it was furnished in exquisite taste. John Siddeley would have given it top marks! She filled me with envy when she took me into a room entirely devoted to built-in wardrobes! As soon as I saw it, I was determined that if I could ever get Sandy to agree, I was one day going to have similar built-in wardrobes with individual compartments for easy storage of variously sized items, like handbags, hats, and shoes. I now had far too many clothes squashed on too few rails, and I guiltily broke the 'thou shalt not covet' commandment that day when I was shown Barbara's solution to such a problem. She even had shelves for jumpers and stockings, not to mention rows of rails for dresses, coats and suits. It was like a fitting room in a large department store, and I could hardly tear myself away.

The rest of the house was a dream of rich jewel colourings, and adorned with magnificent gifts from Hollywood and London, from people whose names would have been starred in any Who's Who of show business. I'd never heard of anybody giving a personal gift as a wedding present. In Springburn, all items were of a practical nature, from linen for the bed (if you were lucky!) down to butter dishes. But Barbara's grandmother gave her a beautiful brooch of gold and uncut rubies, and I was quite dazzled both by the bauble itself and the originality of even thinking of such a thing.

The wedding day was fixed for July 1956, just a little over a year after Bebe and Ben's silver wedding celebrations, and it promised to be another star-studded occasion. As

Russell was of the Protestant faith and Barbara was a Catholic, it was to be a shortened religious service in the beautiful Catholic Church in Spanish Place, which seemed very appropriate with Bebe's Spanish ancestry. There would be a reception afterwards in a well-known suite of rooms opposite Hyde Park, in Park Lane.

Richard Lyon at that time shared a flat with Barbara, and she decided he'd be the perfect guinea pig to try out all her cookery experiments. As he and I were legendary among the cast for always being hungry and yet always being slim, with allegedly hollow legs, Barbara felt sure he would tackle with enthusiasm all the home cooking with which she would later startle Russell. She was determined to be the perfect housewife.

The moment I mentioned a recipe, she would whip out notebook and pencil, and would rush off after rehearsal to try it out. No sooner the word than the blow for our Barbara! One afternoon she heard me mention scallops, and instantly rang up her fishmonger and ordered two dozen to be sent round to the flat. After rehearsal, she went straight home and cooked them in the rich cheese sauce for which I'd given her the recipe, divided them out, then sat back and anxiously awaited Richard's verdict. Poor Richard! Barbara rang me up to report that while she, the maid, Richard's friend and the French poodle had all adored the rich dish, Richard was lying upstairs groaning, sick as a dog!

'Barbara,' I said, scandalized at the waste, and ignoring Richard's delicate condition, 'you didn't give expensive scallops and cheese sauce to a *poodle*!'

'Of course I did,' she said. 'I wasn't going to throw them out and we had too many.'

'But you could have heated them through next day,' I said. 'It would have been quite safe in this weather, so long as you brought them to boiling point again, and didn't overcook them. You don't have to finish everything you cook in one go.'

'I wanted to wash the dish,' she said, as though that explained everything, 'and the poodle loved them and sat up and begged for more.' She giggled at my gasp of outrage. 'The poodle had far better taste than Richard, and really appreciated my cooking.'

In the run-up to the wedding, I began to feel I was in charge of the answering service of *Good Housekeeping*! She'd ring up to check the price of steak in Pinner. She'd want to check how much we paid for having our windows cleaned. She begged to know what the paste ought to look like when she was making chocolate éclairs! 'Barbara,' I protested, 'never mind éclairs at this stage. Concentrate on steak pies, Yorkshire pudding and apple tarts.'

On our shopping expeditions, she wouldn't want to waste a second while I considered the price and quality of my purchases. The moment she'd got what she wanted, she'd tug my arm and say, 'Come on, Molly. We don't want to spend any more time here. I want to see so-and-so in another shop.' This absolutely infuriated me, but I sighed and gave in, and left my purchases for another day when I would be alone. This docile attitude was not characteristic of me, I may say, but I realized that after all she was a bride-to-be, and she had a tremendous amount to do in the little free time we had between recordings. And I remembered my own wild dashing up and down Sauchiehall Street and Buchanan Street in my lunch-hour from the office, when feathering my own wee nest in Glasgow, and tried to be tolerant and understanding!

This meek and mild attitude on my part, though, didn't stop me on the day I saw my chance to let her realize how demanding she'd become. She'd been shopping with Edana Romney, a beautiful actress friend of her parents, and a big name in films and TV at that time, and when she came into rehearsal she came straight over to me and said, 'I'm not going shopping with Edana again. She won't wait a minute after she's got what *she* wants, and I had to leave half the shops we visited without getting what *I* wanted.'

'Barbara,' I said, looking her straight in the eye, 'that's *exactly* what you do to me!'

She was genuinely shocked.

'I don't,' she said. And then, with a hesitant, doubting look, 'Do I?'

When I gave her a detailed recital of our last shopping expedition, including the number of times I'd been tugged away before I could make my own purchases, she threw up her hands in a comical gesture, 'I give in,' she said, 'I give in. Don't let me *do* such a thing again, Molly, for I can see how irritating and selfish it is.'

I felt a bit like my grannie after she'd taught me some home truth. But it wouldn't do Barbara any harm to be aware that there were other folk in the world with their own needs. It's not easy to be the only daughter of a famous couple, and bonnie to boot, for there is a great deal of spoiling which isn't even recognized as such, and she'd have to learn very soon to give and take in the closeness of marriage.

When Barbara's wedding day dawned, golden and sunny and perfect, my mother was on holiday with us and she came into London to savour some of the excitement of the occasion. She was absolutely petrified by the size of the crowds, for the short street was so lined with fans who'd been queuing there since nine o'clock that morning, that the cars couldn't get through. So we had to get out and walk the last few hundred yards.

The crowds surged forward, policemen were pushed over, women fainted, autograph books were thrust under our noses, flash bulbs exploded and the crowd went wild with excitement as they recognized the members of the cast, and began chanting each name as we appeared. 'A . . . ggie, A . . . ggie,' 'Fl . . . orrie, Fl . . . orrie,' 'W . . . imple, W . . . imple,' as helpful police passed us from hand to hand, and managed somehow to get us through the door and into the calm atmosphere of the church, more or less unscathed. My good hat, bought expensively in Liberty's, was right down over my nose by the time I reached the safe haven behind the big door, and the anchoring elastic had shot through my carefully brushed pageboy hair-style, scattering neatness as it went.

It was a strange feeling sitting inside that lovely church, listening to the chanting still going on in the street. Stranger still to look round and see so many faces, known only from the screen till then. Tony Martin, who'd leaped to our notice with his magnificent rendering of *The Tenement Symphony*, Douglas Fairbanks Jr and his wife, the Hulberts, Jack Payne, Louella Parsons, the famous Hollywood gossip columnist, Tyrone Power, Edana Romney who looked just as ravishing as she did on the screen (I wondered if she'd bought her gorgeous lace outfit during one of the shopping expeditions with Barbara!) and a host of writers from films and TV, as well as family friends and relatives.

I was riveted by the jewellery of the guest sitting right in front of me. I didn't know who she was, but her turquoise and diamond necklace was fastened with a circular swirl of precious stones as big as a knuckleduster, and she wore matching turquoise and diamond earrings as large as old-fashioned toffee balls. Against a plain dark dress and softly draped turban, the jewels looked stunning.

I discovered later that she was the wife of a millionaire, with whom Ben and Bebe often spent the weekend. Ben told me once that in spite of all the luxury in their house, the pillows felt as if they were stuffed with rocks, and he couldn't sleep a wink. He'd seriously been tempted to carry his own soft pillows with him after his first visit, but hadn't quite had the nerve! As one who is sensitive even to the hard spine of a feather, Ben had my fullest sympathy and understanding! I always say I'm like the Princess who slept on the pea in this respect.

As I sat mesmerized, gazing at the intricate patterning of the lovely necklace, I became aware that the chanting outside was taking on a different note. Hysteria was rising, and there were screams of excitement and a little panic. It must be Barbara and Ben arriving. Ben told me afterwards that the crowd had surged round the bridal car with such pressure that Barbara couldn't get out. Ben had had to leap ont alone, and from the pavement beg them to move back.

Only then could Barbara in her beautiful lace-edged wedding gown safely make her way up the steps and into the church to become Mrs Russell Turner.

But it didn't work out. The more I saw of them together, as on the occasions when Russell would collect Barbara after our TV rehearsals, and on the evening they had dinner with us in Pinner before we went on to judge a local talent contest, the more I felt that my misgivings were all too clearly justified.

They both tried hard, but they were simply incompatible. It was such a pity, and it was a shattering experience for Barbara against the solid background of the rock-firm relationship of her parents. And when it ended in divorce, Bebe and Ben hid their own heartbreak and helped her through the worst moments.

Once, long afterwards, Barbara asked me if I had ever heard anything in the way of gossip about either of them when the break-up of their marriage was obvious to everyone with eyes to see. I told her, quite truthfully, that I hadn't, but added that for my own part I didn't require to listen to any gossip, for I had thought the marriage might not stand the test of time.

Barbara stared at me. 'But why didn't you tell me?' she cried.

'Barbara,' I answered her quietly, 'would you have listened?' There was a short silence, and when she didn't speak, I added, 'And had I any right to voice my doubts?'

She sighed then. 'No, you're right,' she said, 'I wouldn't have listened.'

And then she smiled when I said, 'But I'll tell you the next time, so just you make sure you pick a winner.'

I could say this now, because I could see that at last she was over the worst.

When she was truly over it, she found happiness with Colin, whom she had grown to know as her accountant, a quiet, steady type, nothing to do with show business. In the fullness of time, they had a little boy, to whom Barbara gave the name of one of Scotland's heroes, Bruce. 'Smart as a whip,' as Ben says, and with a lot of Bebe's magic and loving nature.

Bruce shares one characteristic with me. He never stops talking!

2

Richard Lyon was great fun to work with, and had tremendous talent in the field of light comedy. I remember Jack Hulbert had said at Blackpool that Richard had the makings of an excellent light comedian. Although he hadn't done much in the theatre, I was very struck by the way he could try out scenes and moves in front of an audience, and wasn't in the least thrown by any new 'business' we decided to introduce. He was very easy to work with, and I felt happily relaxed in all the scenes I had with him.

He was mad about photography and about cars. He used to put the fear of death in me by seizing my hand at the end of our TV rehearsals, running me to his sports car, pushing me in, and roaring at top speed along the Strand towards Trafalgar Square, occasionally standing up to wave to passers-by! There would be shouts of, 'Oh, there's Master Richard with Aggie,' and the traffic would come to a standstill for a moment or so, as people ran to get a closer look.

Doris Rogers (Florrie) used to say to me, 'I wouldn't get into Richard Lyon's car if you paid me a fortune.' She was an excellent driver (as was Richard) and strongly disapproved of his larking about. 'But I've no option, Doris,' I'd say weakly, 'I don't like to hurt his feelings by utterly refusing to take a lift to the station.'

But it wasn't larking at all which caused his accident. It was sheer dead tiredness. We'd just finished a long TV season, and were all about to set off on our various holidays to recharge the batteries before the start of the radio series which was to follow.

Richard had gone back to his home with Jill Ireland, for a bite of supper, and they'd sat quietly listening to gramophone records until nearly midnight, when he got the car out to drive Jill home. Jill was a very pretty blonde starlet whom he adored, and when they weren't together in person, they were on the phone non-stop. In fact often if he had to go for clothes fittings for our TV series and wasn't able to get back in time for their daily phone call, I was deputed to ring Jill to tell her that he hadn't returned but would call the moment he got in.

The roads were quiet as he drove Jill towards her home that night, and he could only conclude later that he had closed his eyes for a second. For the next thing he knew the car was bouncing off one of the huge trees which lined the road, and was being rocked upside down. Richard has fantastically fast reactions. I think this was one of the things we shared and which we recognized in one another. But I could never have shown his cool resource in such paralysingly frightening circumstances. In that split second when he saw what was happening, his first instinct was to switch off the engine, so that the car wouldn't catch fire and the petrol ignite, and the next swift reaction was to protect Jill's lovely face, which he caught with his other hand and pushed down towards the floor, away from the glass windscreen.

When they got them out, the only damage Jill sustained was a bruised ankle where it had been knocked against the handbrake, but Richard had severe concussion, cuts and bruises, and was in the London Clinic for weeks.

When I saw the cuts I could have wept, and I remembered so clearly Bebe's warning when Richard had been showing her brochures for new cars before he'd bought that model. She had looked up at him earnestly and had said, 'Richard, you must always be very careful. You can do so much damage to yourself and others and it only needs one stupid mistake to ruin your looks and your health for good.'

I had been very impressed by that conversation, for I didn't often hear Bebe speak seriously about anything outside the script, and the scene had imprinted itself on my mind, like a photograph. Bebe, her huge dark eyes lifted to her son, who stood with one arm round her shoulder where she sat with the brochure spread out on the table in front of her, and Richard, with eyes only for the illustrated model of the car he intended to buy.

But the accident had one unexpected side effect. At that time Americans had to do military service, and Richard had been passed A1 and was supposed to go out to the States to fulfil his duties. To keep the cast with a young male in it to provide the teenage interest, a young actor Richard Bellaers had been booked, as a pretend cousin of Richard and Barbara, and his part would be built up more and more after Richard left so that the programme would again have a nice young balance.

Now, with this accident, Richard's military service was cancelled, and he wouldn't be leaving the cast. I think Bebe felt everything was mixed with mercy! And perhaps God was keeping the Lyon family together, whatever the Army may have planned!

So he wouldn't be leaving us, and I wondered what would happen to poor Richard Bellaers. However, all was well, for the public had taken to him, and liked him, and it made a nice abrasive teenage situation with the two Richards in cahoots either with or against Barbara, or the rest of us, as the scripts dictated.

But it wasn't the return of our own Richard which pushed the other Richard out. It was anno domini!

We returned at the end of the summer holidays, congregating at the Lyons' house in Southwick Street for a read-through and a get-together. The moment young Bellaers said 'Hullo, Molly' to me, I knew that was the end of his career. His voice had dropped to a deep bass-baritone, about the level of Ben's, and he sounded like our Richard's pop. 'Richard Bellaers,' I said to him solemnly, 'you're out, son!' 'But why?' he asked me tremulously. I wanted to warn him before the blow fell, for I know only too well how shattering the truth is when it has to be faced unexpectedly.

So I told him that in radio it is the *sound* which matters, and he didn't sound like a youngster any more. He was still only fifteen, or thereabouts, but the voice didn't paint a picture of a young lad who hadn't seen a razor. 'You've been brought into the series to be a lively "Just William" type of little boy, Richard,' I said, 'and I'm afraid with the disappearance of the little boy's voice, goes the disappearance of the character.'

I advised him not to try to use a falsetto voice, for if he wanted to go on as an actor he would ruin his true voice.

Sure enough, when we went on to the read-through, with poor young Richard keeping his jaws clamped till that moment so that nobody but myself would realize what had happened, there was instant horror when Bebe and Ben heard him say his lines. The rehearsal came to a full stop while the lad tried various falsetto registers, which all came out in cracked squeaks.

That was the end of 'Cousin Richard', and the last I heard of him was that he was working for B O A C where his beautiful deep voice could only be a positive asset. He was a nice lad, and made a real niche for himself during the short time he was with us.

But if his disappointment was hard for him to bear, it was nothing to the heartbreak our own Richard now had to suffer. He was still head over heels in love with Jill, who was just then in the throes of a big film over at Pinewood Studios. On the Monday of that week, a new young actor was due to start work on the picture, David McCallum, the son of *the* McCallum, whom we Scots were very proud of as leader of the Philharmonic Orchestra. Unknown to any of us, and that included Richard, Jill and David had fallen in love at first sight, and by the end of the week they'd taken out a special licence and were married!

At her mother's insistence, Jill had been forced to find the courage to ring Richard to let him know before the reporters did. But the rest of us only learned of the whirlwind romance and marriage when we opened our newspapers on the way to our rehearsal. I didn't know how to face Richard. I knew the extent of his feeling, and I felt sick.

I didn't go into the rehearsal room until just before the time for the read-through, and I never raised my eyes from my script until it was finished. Everyone was very quiet, but Bebe and Ben, with superb professional detachment, behaved completely normally, except that there were no fun and games.

As I moved over to the table to mark my alterations, Richard was by my side. 'Did you read about Jill?' I heard him say. I lifted my eyes to his face. It was as white as chalk, and the eyes were blank. I wanted to burst into tears.

'Yes, I did, Richard. I'm so sorry.' And then, of course, I added the usual platitudes that it was better to find out now than later. He was in an anguish of regret that he hadn't married her a year earlier, but it had been thought wiser then to give it a little time to let Barbara's marriage settle down before both of them had to be presented as wedded 'children'. This was the high price to be paid because they were all playing themselves, and not fictitious characters. Their real lives and activities had to be woven into the script and the timing of such important matters as marriage had to be taken into consideration.

It hadn't seemed a matter of life and death to have to wait for one short year before he could take his bride to the altar. Nobody could have foreseen what Fate had in store, and what a chance meeting would bring.

I quoted Miss Chree's words, to comfort him. 'If she be not fair to me, what care I *how* fair she be?' and hoped he would find somebody far more stable, whom he could love and who would love him and appreciate his qualities. He did. He found Angela, a delightful blonde dancer, one of a large family, with a Cornish background, who looked like the sugar plum fairy but had the most practical head screwed on her pretty shoulders. When they became engaged, Bebe won Angela's love forever when she said to her, 'If Richard had asked me to go out and find him a wife,

I would have picked you.' I can't think of any words more guaranteed to ensure the happiest of mother-in-law—daughter-in-law relationships, and when the children, Penny and Timothy, came along to make Bebe a grandmother, happiness was complete.

Richard used to laugh at me because I still travelled to town by train, and didn't use the little Morris car I'd learnt to drive. 'Molly buys a car and keeps it in the garage,' he'd announce to all and sundry, 'she's scared it'll get wet.'

It was true I hadn't the courage to face the London-bound traffic, but it was thanks to my excitement over my first long solo drive in the other direction that I got one of my biggest and most enjoyable film parts. I had been asked to go along to be seen by the American director of a re-make of the Scottish film *Jeannie*, now to be called *Let's be Happy*, starring Vera Ellen and Tony Martin (whom I'd last seen at Barbara's wedding), with Robert Flemyng as the Scottish Laird.

To get to the studios I'd have to drive through about ten or so miles of twisting, narrow lanes and busy main roads from Pinner, and although Sandy was nervous about my driving alone through unknown territory, I was determined to use the car. The journey by public transport was nightmarish, and would have made punctuality for the interview very difficult, and I knew if I were lucky enough to get the part I could make my life much easier by driving myself cross-country on filming days.

Sandy got the car out for me, and waved me off with much the same expression he might have used had I been setting off to walk on the moon!

Normally any interview has me churned up with nervous tension, with my mind almost guaranteed to go a blank when the question is put, 'And what have you done, Miss Weir?' This time it was entirely different. I was so excited at having successfully negotiated the road journey in my own little car, under my own steam, even having parked it safely without damage to life or limb, that I burst into the director's office with exultant cries of, 'I've driven here myself. Isn't it marvellous? It's the first time I've been out in the car alone.'

I think the man really thought I was a nut case, or possibly he put it down to the unpredictable behaviour of a Scot, but it certainly broke the ice.

Within seconds we were swopping tales of our cars, our home backgrounds, our families, the best golf courses he ought to play over before he returned to America, in fact everything but the film itself.

After we'd had coffee and had been about half half an hour together, he looked up and smiled, 'Well, Miss Weir. What about this part, do you want it?'

'Of course,' I answered, knowing nothing about it except that I was supposed to be the flower-seller at the flower boutique in the Caledonian Hotel in Edinburgh. But if the director thought I was right, then that was good enough for me.

'Well then, what are we waiting for?' he chuckled. 'The part's yours.'

And that was that.

My mother was down once more for her summer holiday, and she was as excited as I was at the prospect of my working with Vera Ellen, whom she greatly admired, as we all did, as a superb dancer. 'My goodness, she has such a wee waist, ye could span it wi' your two hands,' my mother commented admiringly. She also had a lovely golden ponytail which I envied, and long, long legs which were apparently tireless.

She had recently married a handsome rich young American oil executive, and they were very much in love. They couldn't bear to be apart, and he used to fly over from the States every few days to see her – just as I might pop up and down to Glasgow, and he would sit and watch her with loving concentration as she went through her dance routines.

He kept a devoted watch to see that she didn't overtire herself, for she was a real perfectionist, like Bebe, and would dance till she dropped. Some days she seemed like a leggy schoolgirl who'd outgrown her strength, with her fine slender figure, whirling coltish legs, golden ponytail and her pale, pale, face. But this 'schoolgirl' was a world star.

I was fascinated to watch her rich tycoon husband sitting on an upturned box hour after hour, saying very little, but just being there so that when his talented wife wanted support, they could flash each other a loving smile and know the other was near. Very romantic I found this, as well as exciting.

I found Tony Martin to be great fun, and a terrible tease, a bit like Ben Lyon. And, believe it or not, I won his friendship by not saying a single word – well, to begin with that is!

I think my reputation as a gasbag had gone before me. Either that or the director feared I'd erupt on to the set with the same excitement I'd shown when I had that first interview with him. Anyway, for whatever reason I was warned by the front office that I was not to start chatting during meal breaks. The stars required a lot of rest to recover from the strain and heat of the set. They might want to be quiet and wouldn't wish to be rude and shut me up! They were sure I realized a peaceful atmosphere at meal times was essential, and there was no need whatsoever to attempt to be social and indulge in tiring chit-chat!

On the first day I was called to stand-by for filming, in case they reached my scene, I was sent off to the canteen early for lunch. Sitting alone was Tony Martin. Although I'd seen him at Barbara's wedding, I knew he would certainly not remember seeing me there and, remembering the instructions about exhausted stars, I took a seat at the far end of the room. There the two of us sat, in utter silence, in an otherwise vast empty canteen. I was terrified to open my mouth, except to eat my lunch, so I got on with my meal, hardly daring even to make a noise as I laid down my knife and fork.

I hoped my stomach wouldn't rumble, and I began to pray that somebody else would come in to relieve what to me was a nerve-racking and embarrassing silence. Nobody did. So I ploughed on with the biscuits and cheese, hoping I looked more at ease than I felt.

Seeing I had made no attempt either to speak to him or to join him, *he* broke the silence and said how nice it was to find some quietness. Then, hearing my Scots accent, he asked if he could join me!

That was the beginning of a jolly friendship, which found me doing most of the listening, for Tony talked about the great Hollywood names as we would refer to our nextdoor neighbours. Not in any sense of name-dropping, but just as casually as we'd speak of close chums, which they were in his world.

I was particularly intrigued to hear about a regular Christmas Eve party which was thrown jointly because several of the friends shared the same birthday. There would be the Bogarts, the James Stewarts, the Astaires, Tony and his lovely wife, Cyd Charisse, maybe Edward G. Robinson and several others, and after the toasting and the meal they'd all separate around midnight, because the family men were anxious to get home to fill the children's stockings.

I found this a most unexpected and endearing side of those top Hollywood stars and felt that never again would I look at any of them up there on the silver screen, without imagining the private family side of their lives, and realizing they went home to bed at night, just like me.

I was also intrigued to find inside a film star of the magnitude of Tony Martin, a real outdoor man interested in all sports. I'd always been told that to get to the top you had to have a one-track mind, with no time for anything outside the career. He was, I found, an extremely devoted family man, and of course a splendid singer. All that rich volume of sound in *The Tenement Symphony* was not faked by the engineers. It all came from him. I know. For my dressing room was over his, and as he practised every day, I felt these were private concert performances for my special delight. I little thought when I first heard that marvellous song in the cinema in Glasgow, that the day would dawn when I'd hear it all by myself practically daily from that golden throat.

As far as my part in our film was concerned, he was a great leg-puller and a terrible tease.

Although I appeared in a great many scenes as 'background', I hadn't actually very much dialogue. So the director decided he would shoot all my talking scenes in one segment at any suitable time during a scene-change.

Every morning when I reported to the studio, Tony would greet me with the words, 'Today's the day, Molly. Yup, today they're gonna let you speak. Don't worry, honey, we'll all be in there rootin' for you.'

But somehow that dialogue sequence was continually postponed. Even when it was scheduled to be done, something else turned up which was considered more important, and I'd be told yet again, 'Well, maybe later.'

It became a huge joke, and I grew more and more nervous at the very idea of saying words in the presence of the mocking Tony and the clever Robert Flemyng. Not to mention Vera Ellen.

On a day when I wasn't even 'on call', but just on 'stand-by', the great moment arrived, and it was Tony who made sure that I knew all about it. And that everybody else did too!

He called for silence on the set.

Everybody stopped talking, right down to the last carpenter.

'*Okay*, fellows – this is it!' he announced. 'I want all you guys to pay close attention to Miss Weir. It's what we've all been waiting for – an object lesson in dialogue which could well win her an Oscar!'

Everybody enjoyed the joke, except me. For I was the one who had to do the thing, with everybody watching and listening.

Just as I was about to say my piece, Tony interrupted once more. Striking a melodramatic pose, he pointed to me with quivering finger and intoned, 'She *speaks*!'

The whole studio dissolved in laughter.

I don't know how I managed to get those first words out, but I did, and Tony led the applause at the end. For that first piece of immortal prose consisted of the words, 'Thank you, m'Lord,' to Robert Flemyng.

But underneath all that badinage Tony Martin was a kind and considerate actor, for when it came to my dialogue scene with him, he made sure that the lighting favoured me, and I had the lion's share of the camera. I had worked long enough in show business by this time to know such un-selfishness is a very rare quality in an actor, and I never forgot his generosity and his friendship.

But it was Robert Flemyng who taught me a great deal about keeping a calm attitude (or calm sooch, as we'd say in Scotland) in the face of the irritations of the film world.

He had arrived on the set one morning in full Highland dress, looking as if he'd just stepped out of a picture frame. Splendid in every respect. Just as we were all voicing our admiration, the assistant director rushed over. 'Oh, I'm so sorry, Mr Flemyng, I've made a mistake. The next scene requires you to be in your lounge suit.'

Without the least sign of irritation, Robert took the long walk across the set, went upstairs to his dressing room where he removed all that complicated Highland attire, and returned in his Savile Row lounge suit. As he was playing a Lord, he had to be dressed in keeping with his position.

He had just come through the door when the assistant director ran over to him again. 'I'm *terribly* sorry, Mr Flemyng, but we can't get the set ready in time. I'm afraid it will have to be the Highland dress after all.'

I waited for the explosion.

None came.

There wasn't a flicker of emotion as Robert turned, and in the same leisurely fashion headed in the direction of his dressing room, where the lounge suit was exchanged for the Highland outfit.

When he came back, I said, 'Robert! *Three* outfits within the space of half an hour. Aren't you spitting mad?'

'My dear child,' he smiled in his lazy, charming manner, 'I realized long ago that the film world was a madhouse, and the only way to keep one's sanity is to do what one is told to do and question nothing. Once you start to fume and fret over delays, and little mistakes over costume, you're finished. Just keep an eye on the lovely, lovely money, enjoy the work, and take it all as it comes.'

It was the best advice I'd heard since my theatre days when dear Marjorie Fielding had told me never to waste energy regretting jobs once they'd been turned down,* and ever since that happy film I've tried to follow Robert's wise philosophy when things might otherwise have tended to make me 'lose the heid'.

One day Tony's wife, Cyd Charisse, came in, on her way back to America from Paris, where she had been filming. Tall, distinguished-looking in a very English way with her beautiful tweed overcoat, she was also very, very tired after weeks of energetic dancing for the movie. It was a great thrill to see two of Hollywood's best dancers chatting together on our set, and again I had to rub my eyes to make sure it wasn't all a dream, and that Cyd and Vera Ellen were really there.

I still couldn't get over speaking and eating with stars who had until then been ten times larger than life up there on the screen. Any more than I could get over the fact that they weren't the least bit surprised to see me among them pretending to be an actress! I wonder if they secretly felt as astonished as I did by it all?

When the film ended, I took an enormous bunch of blue hydrangeas to Vera Ellen, from our garden. She was flatteringly amazed to know I'd grown them myself, for they are considered a very exotic bloom in her part of America. She filled two buckets with them and said she was going to take them back to the Dorchester to let them see just what blue hydrangeas ought to look like! They *were* fine specimens, although I say it myself, and you will gather that I do not exaggerate when I tell you that even the

*A Toe on the Ladder

curator of the local park asked me for cuttings, as he couldn't achieve anything like their quality or colour in the park under his care.

My mother was thrilled to know Vera Ellen had accepted flowers from our garden. 'Aye,' she said happily, 'she'd have had to pey braw saut for a' thae flooers if she'd bought them in the shops.' In Springburn all flowers had to be bought, for nobody in the tenements had a garden, and my mother could never get over the sheer quantities of blossoms it was possible to give from one's own garden, and hardly notice their absence. She had been utterly dismayed one day when she saw me filling two newspapers with two dozen full-blown roses for an old lady who'd stood admiring them at the gate. 'Ye shouldnae gi'e a' yer flooers away like that,' she'd admonished. 'But, mother, there will be dozens to take their place tomorrow. At this time of the year, they've to be cut every day.' She didn't believe me, but next day when she went out to the garden, the miracle had taken place, and she said, 'Aye, the auld sowl would be pleased wi' her roses, if she had enough vases fur them, and we've got plenty mair where they came from.'

This was a bounty which seemed endless, and our garden was a constant joy to her.

It was just as well that my mother could be happily left to her own company in the quiet beauty of the garden, for although I always tried to be free of commitments while she was with us, this wasn't always possible. And that particular year I had another most original and exciting job offered to me.

The Queen was on her first tour of New Zealand, and the newsreels were flown into London every night, for processing, and dubbing, to be shown as a travelogue a little later in all the main cinemas throughout the world. One day the telephone rang, and it was Castleton Knight, a famous name in the newsreel world, and he wanted to know if I would come to see him to discuss the possibility of my doing the commentary and playing the 'voices' of Scottish farmers' wives who appeared in scenes with the Queen.

My mother came into London with me, and had a nice wander through Liberty's shop while I was at the interview, and was agog to hear all my news when I joined her for a delicious lunch in a little favourite buttery off Bond Street. 'By jings,' she said, 'wait till ah tell the neebors you're to be in Topical Budget!' All newsreels were Topical Budget to my mother, whether they were Pathétone, Movietone, or whatever.

But she was aghast when she heard that it would be 'night-shift' work, and I'd be out from ten o'clock at night, until the next morning, for the newsreels couldn't reach the end of the processing stage until almost my normal bedtime. It was the strangest assignment I'd ever had; but fascinating.

A car came and took me to the studios, and with Castleton Knight and another technician I sat around, or I should say lounged around on a blissfully comfortable settee, chatting and eating bacon and eggs and drinking endless cups of coffee, until each reel was ready. Then we'd go through to the recording studio, the film would be run through on the projection screen, and I'd do the commentary, or play the farm wifie's voice if she was involved, and we'd work on it until it all matched perfectly.

The most famous 'name behind the voice' was Bob Danvers Walker, and I was at last seeing this man, whose unmistakable tones had boomed forth from movie newsreels for years in the big cinemas. I watched him like a hawk, to learn all I could of this new technique, and it was fascinating to be there and hear it all at first hand, with the flesh and blood man right there in front of me, and actually playing some scenes *with* me.

We only did one reel at a time, and there were hours of waiting until the next one was ready.

I was delivered back to the house at 6.30 a.m. and found Sandy sitting snoozing in the front room with the light on, never having been in bed all night, in case he'd have to come out to collect me! He didn't trust film people an inch to provide cars once they'd finished with the work! But they hadn't finished, for I had to go back several times, and repeat this night-shift stint, so they spoilt me beautifully by providing transport on each occasion.

I was vexed with Sandy for losing his sleep, but he was so pleased to see me back safely, as was my mother, that he didn't even look bleary-eyed. They had a bacon-and-egg breakfast while I told them all about the night's work. I couldn't look at another egg, having had about three nocturnal breakfasts between 'takes'.

It made a beautiful colour film, and one of the most amusing incidents happened when we went to see it ourselves at the Leicester Square cinema in London. When the farm scenes came on, a lady behind us said to her friend, 'What a nice Scottish voice that farmer's wife has. I didn't realize they spoke like that in New Zealand!'

'Oh yes,' said her companion, 'it's a well-known fact that thousands of Scots emigrated to Australia and New Zealand and you'll find that accent all over both countries.'

I was delighted to find that there was complete acceptance of the voice as belonging to the lady on the farm, so the dubbing must have been convincing.

And when I heard the warm strong tones of Bob Danvers Walker later on in the film, I could see us again sitting devouring bacon and eggs during the long hours of waiting, and could hardly believe we could sound so wide-awake and lively when the work was done on 'night-shift'.

It had been a 'once-in-a-lifetime' job, and my one regret was that in real life I never ever got so close to our beloved Queen as I did when I was a voice on that newsreel.

3

That was a busy summer, and my mother had to be left again to the tranquillity of the garden while I went down to Southampton TV studios to do a spot in Jim Dale's live lunchtime show. David Manderson, who was in charge of the studios there at that time, knew I was interested in cooking, for he'd heard me on *Woman's Hour*, and he also knew I could be trusted to take part in any sketches which required a comedy touch, so he invited me to take a main part in the programme by demonstrating cookery!

Now it's one thing cooking in your own kitchen, but it's quite another when you have to cook in front of a live audience in the studio, plus millions looking into their TV sets, and keep up a lively running commentary while you mix, whip, roll out and bake.

It was nerve-racking, to say the least, but it was a challenge and as always if anybody asked me to do anything, it seemed cowardly to refuse. So, armed with my pans and my tins and list of ingredients, I set off for Southampton. I stayed at a little guest house overnight, to be ready for a crack of dawn start, and I was awake half the night working out all the things I'd have to do in preparation for the programme.

The first thing to be attended to was the list of ingredients, which I handed to a lad, who went down to the shops and bought everything. The minute he returned, I was at it, full speed ahead, until virtually the moment the audience came in. I had to have three lots of everything. For the lemon meringue pie, say, I had to have a blind pastry case baked to show to the audience. I had to have the filling made to show as well. I had to make a complete pie and bake it, so that I could produce it at the end of the programme, to let everyone see what it ought to look like. I had also to have a third lot of ingredients in their unprepared state, to let everyone see me actually making the dish.

On top of all this cooking, I had to rehearse the sketches if I was required, have my face made up, and my hair, and get into my clothes in readiness for the audience arrival by 12.30. It was absolutely hell-for-leather. All cookery programmes have had my unbounded admiration ever since.

But once I'd got over my terror, there was a lot of fun too. Everyone is interested in cookery, and there was no trouble in catching the audience's attention, for they were mostly women. The studio lads, too, were rapt and silent, licking their lips in the knowledge that they'd be eating what I cooked for their lunch that day! I never saw such a rush at the end of the programme. They were into that oven and away with the cake or the pie or the scones before I could turn round to say, 'Help yourselves.' Well, at least they showed they had no doubts that it was all going to be worth eating!

Jim Dale was extremely clever, and versatile, and had a lovely warm way with an audience. I couldn't understand why he wasn't a big name in the West End, for he had obviously enormous talent. But at that time he was mostly connected in the public mind with singing, and it wasn't until he turned to legitimate theatre that he roared to success, and became a member of the National Theatre, and the Young Vic, and toured America in Shakespeare. His song-writing won him an Oscar, and as I write he goes from success to success with the Young Vic. I find it a great joy to have recognized this talent from the start.

It was stimulating for me to take part in the sketches with him and the dancers, and I remember in one scene we had to do a cod version of Scottish country dancing. I was doing it fairly light-heartedly, for it was all a sort of mad romp, but I suppose when one has had a childhood spent doing Scottish dancing properly, one's feet and posture naturally fall into accustomed movements. When it was all over, and we'd exited panting and laughing to enthusiastic audience applause, David Manderson said to me, regretfully, 'When I see you doing Scottish dancing properly like that, Molly, so light on your feet, I so wish I'd sent the children to Scottish dancing. It's such an asset.'

I was genuinely astonished. I'd really only been larking about, and I was flattered beyond words that David had actually found my capering light and graceful. I wished my Highland dancing teacher from Garngad could have heard his words, for she it was who gave me the rudiments of the light Scottish style of pas-de-bas, and who despairingly decided my feet were all right, if only I would learn to dance on the one spot and not always end up in her fireplace!

I did about half a dozen of those programmes all told, and I think my mother quite enjoyed taking charge of the house for twenty-four hours, although I was faintly alarmed by seeing how nervous she had grown over preparing food. Even the simplest mince and potatoes seemed to present difficulties, and I hoped she wasn't living on tea and biscuits at home. 'No, no,' she assured me, 'I eat fine. I make soup nearly every day, and I have a wee bit of lemon sole when I feel like it, and a chop or a piece of chicken.' I believed her, although I wondered why then she was so agitated over cooking for herself and Sandy. But it was maybe just because it *was* for Sandy as well as herself, for she had maybe grown away from catering for two.

Mark you, I could understand anyone alone eating very sparingly, for I myself adopt utterly different eating habits when I've only myself to cook for. Cold ham or tongue with a tomato for lunch, and an egg or piece of fish or a pie for tea, could keep me going for weeks. And yet, when there are two of us, you'd think I was feeding a regiment from the amount of cooking and baking I do. I always remember in Orchard Park when I was first married, the workmen saying I should have had a navvy and six kids to feed, with my enthusiasm for cookery and my busy baking sessions. 'Why,' I asked them wonderingly, 'don't all the women cook like me?' 'Them!' came the scornful reply. 'They maistly live oot o' tins. You've only got to look in their rubbish bins to tell that!' I was very surprised at such an extravagant way of living, for my mother's and my grannie's teaching had made me regard tinned food as emergency catering, or for high days and holidays. Not for everyday living.

They'd made me equally careful with my clothes, and I never sat about in my good suits or dresses, but changed into work-a-day garments the minute I got home. I loved fashion, although I may not have looked like it, caught in working trousers and pullover, and I was thrilled beyond measure when Joan Gilbert, then a top TV personality who had a daily Diary which was watched by millions, asked me to model clothes for her show. She was publicizing a new idea in sizing, where the same styled dress or coat or suit was to be presented from the smallest adult size to the largest outsize, to show how identical fashionable lines could be worn whatever the measurements of the wearer. In other words, there was no need for bantams like me to have to scour the children's departments for something to fit me with consequent lack of fashion touches, or the outsize ladies to wear frumpy 'grannie' styles just because they were generously curved.

There were five of us, me being the smallest, right up to a Junoesque lady with a 44 inch bust, all wearing the same styled clothes. Yana, the popular and lovely blonde singer, was also modelling with us. I think she had actually done modelling in her earlier days, and all the others had modelled professionally. I was the only enthusiastic amateur! I think Joan just asked me because I'd done a chat show with her some weeks before, and we got on well together, and I was also smaller than any of the professional adult models on anyone's books.

It was hilarious prancing out there, to the manner born, twirling, opening my coat, slipping out of my sleeves to show the dress, walking back and forth, turning up the collar, and aping all the gestures I'd seen so often when watching a dress show.

Yana got so carried away when it came to her turn, that she forgot to listen to the commentary, and was still doing dainty pirouettes when the next girl ought to have been coming on. In the end, as she was deaf to all hissed instructions to come off, an attendant slithered on all fours across the floor out of camera range and yanked at Yana's petticoat, which came off in her hand, floated down on top of her crouching form and blotted her out like a cloud from heaven!

Yana jumped, gazed down at the shrouded figure at her feet in comic surprise, and then with a radiant smile moved out of camera.

She fell into my arms, dissolved in hysterical laughter, in which I joined. We couldn't move for laughing, and somebody pushed us into the dressing room out of reach of the microphone, where our cackling could do no harm.

Yana still sobbed with laughter. 'Oh, Molly,' she spluttered, 'I didn't *know* anybody was there till I felt my petticoat coming down.' And we'd go into helpless giggles all over again. How we got through the rest of the show I'll never know.

Meantime Joan Gilbert, with superb control, was carrying on with the programme, just as I had seen her do on an unforgettable occasion when old Matty (A. E. Matthews) had been her guest, and had refused point blank to leave the stage, but had held on to her hand and said, 'Oh, never mind about all those people out there. It's a long time since a pretty woman has been so interested in me!' Matty was well into his seventies at that time, and his eccentricity endeared him to the vast TV audience, who were more accustomed to correct behaviour or palsied terror from players facing the cameras for the first time.

One of the treasured stories enjoyed by all of us was the tale of Sybil Thorndike's husband, Lewis Casson, in his first TV play, suddenly finding his mind had gone blank and he couldn't remember a line of his next speech. Instead of goggling like a goldfish, making it obvious to everyone watching what had happened, he had, with breathtaking resource, simply kept his mouth opening and shutting and made it appear that it was the sound which had broken down! No doubt he had had to cope with every emergency in the theatre, and he had simply risen to the occasion when disaster threatened on this newer medium. A marvellous tale! I hoped I could prove as resourceful if ever the occasion demanded, but I very much doubted it. Half a century's experience is a great help at such moments!

However, nothing is much help when you are met with silence when you expect joyous laughter. The BBC decided on an experiment, and thought it would be a stimulating idea to take the top variety radio shows to the regions, to let the main cities have a look at their radio characters in the flesh. For the Lyons, they had chosen Glasgow. Doris Rogers, Horace Percival and I hated flying, so while the others went up by plane we travelled by overnight train. It was simply perishing, with little heating in our coach, and we arrived in Glasgow coughing and sneezing. Ben thought we were quite mad, for as an Air Force officer in the war, he used planes the way I used tramcars in Glasgow, and he always told me, 'Honey, you're out of your mind. You're in far greater danger in a car. Do you think they're going to risk a million bucks' worth of plane? The pilot's got a stake in safety too, you know.'

He had the last laugh when they arrived fresh as daisies, and we three were cold, snuffling and miserable. The chemist provided soothing linctus for me, and Vick for my chest. Bebe gave me a great tip which I've used to this day, although it sounded so daft it might have been a line from the script. 'Rub it on your feet, Aggie,' she urged me, 'I always did this with Richard when he was a little boy, and it cured his cold quicker than anything.' It did too, as I found out.

Glasgow BBC were agog with excitement and pleasure at having been chosen as the city to receive the Lyons, and by the strangest coincidence our producer was called Ben Lyons, a quietly enthusiastic and dedicated man who did everything to put the whole resources of the Corporation at Bebe and Ben's disposal. Nothing was too much trouble, and they were charmed with the supporting cast he had booked for the show. I, of course, was also delighted, for they were my two old friends from radio days in Scotland, Willie Joss and Madeleine Christie.

To give the show a Scottish touch, Bebe had used the name of her own father, a Scot, for one of the jokes, and she expected gales of laughter when this line was spoken. To her amazement and dismay, there was nothing but stony silence. None of us could understand it, and although it made no difference to the rest of the script which Bebe played with superb timing and attack, as did Ben, I could sense an edginess in them, wondering what had gone wrong. Only at the end of the show did we discover that a man of that name had just that day been sentenced to hang for murder!

No wonder there had been silence. It must have seemed to the audience a tasteless use of the name of a condemned man.

My mother was in the audience, and delighted Richard by seizing him to her bosom, and planting a huge kiss on each cheek. She was definitely getting used to show business!

Doris and I were staying at the Spa Hotel, which sent Doris into hysterics because of all the medical paraphernalia lying around, for the treatment of various rheumatic ailments. We had to stay near the BBC, which was why I wasn't at my mother's house, for we didn't know when rehearsals would be called and it was essential to be within walking distance of the studios.

They always say eavesdroppers never hear any good of themselves, and this was amply demonstrated when I overheard two of the waitresses talking in the kitchen when I came down to breakfast.

'Molly Weir's in the dining room,' called one to the other.
'I know, I've seen her,' came the reply.

'Whit do you think of her?' asked the first voice.

'I'm very disappointed in her,' I heard.

My heart sank. I was getting so used to basking in approval by this time, that such criticism fairly ca'ed the feet from me.

'Whit's up wi' her?' demanded the first voice.

I was listening with unashamed interest by this time, ignoring the porridge rapidly cooling on my plate.

'Och, she's far wee-er than I expected. I juist never thocht she would be as wee an' insignificant as that.'

So much for the old Scots saying, 'Good gear goes into sma' bulk.'

Served me right for listening. And there was nothing like a home truth for knocking the conceit out of a body!

But I had a great laugh from the hotel manager when he told me a true tale, which has so much of the old Glasgow in its humour, that I even had the great Billy Connolly curled up with laughter when I told it to him a year or so ago. He promised he wouldn't use it in his act, but he did tell it privately to Richard Burton when they were on a film together, and Burton had relished it too, with great shouts of laughter.

Apparently the manager had a wee Glasgow chap who came to wash and polish his car every Saturday morning, a job he did for years and for which he was paid the sum of seven-and-sixpence. A nice wee chap, as the manager described him, but under-sized. In fact what we in Glasgow would call with affectionate realism, 'A right wee bauchle.'

Well, the wee man died suddenly and the manager thought it would only be seemly for him to go along to pay his respects, for he'd been a faithful worker and had turned out in all weathers, grateful for this little job which gave him his weekend pocket money.

So the manager had gone along to a room-and-kitchen tenement flat in the old Gorbals, in his best dark suit, and had been shown into the room, where all the mourners were seated round the wall on hard chairs, not uttering a word to one another. Hands folded on laps, they'd gazed at him solemnly, no doubt wondering where on earth he had come from.

As he stood by the window, wondering what to say, a face had appeared round the room door, topped by a flat bunnet. 'Ah'm the corpse's brother,' the man said, 'and ah'd like ye a' tae come through tae the kitchen tae drink his health.'

Without a word or a sign of surprise, the entire company followed him through to the kitchen.

The Spa manager told me he was in an agony, trying to suppress his laughter.

As an example of 18-carat gold Glasgow humour, that story is, in my opinion, a classic.

After our recording in the Glasgow studios, we had a fine example of Glasgow hospitality when Madeleine Christie invited all of us to come along to her flat for some supper. She lived not far from the BBC and it was a delightful way to end the evening.

Eddie Fraser was there, and although he had risen to the position of Head of BBC Light Entertainment, was happy to recall the fun we'd shared when we were both appearing in the Pantheon Club's musical productions. He remembered with particular pleasure *Desert Song*, where I played Susan to his Bennie. I always had a feeling that much as Eddie enjoyed the security of an administrative position, his heart was really in the excitement of being a performer.

It was a splendid party of reminiscence and fun and Ben and Bebe were most impressed with this unexpected hospitality, and talked of it for years.

My voice just lasted for the duration of the show, and by next morning had disappeared entirely. It was a combination of cold, excitement, rehearsals, and a party. And the next six days saw me swallowing linctus, rubbing my chest with camphorated oil, and the soles of my feet with Vick, in order to get my sound-box back in good fettle for the next week's radio performance.

I always had the feeling that I was the only actress who had secret worries about her voice. Over-using our vocal chords as we did, because we had to work through colds, bronchial infections, laryngitis, tonsillitis, the lot, they became very vulnerable to particular stresses, and on radio where the slightest flaw was apparent to the listener, it often became a nightmare wondering if the voice would crack or vanish at the worst moment during a gag. One never mentioned such fears to anyone. Nobody wanted to be reminded of his own hidden fears, so we all kept up this fiction that we had cast-iron throats.

But privately I sought the help of a recommended voice coach, poured out my troubles into his sympathetic if expensive ear, and began a course of lessons which were devised to exercise every part of my throat. He was Italian, and just what I needed, for he hadn't the slightest sympathy for imagined vocal-chord failure. When I'd come to a sound which I just *knew* was going to crack my voice, he would thump the piano, and shout, 'Oh yes, darlink, there eet ees, your voice, lying over there eeen the fireplace. Now come on, sing *out, out, out*, wizout fear.'

And I would do it, and all would be well.

But what reassured me more than anything was to see the important and well-known clients, stars from musicals, who also needed his assistance. It was like a draught of pure mountain air to realize I was not the only one, just as it had been when I first went into the theatre fearful of my small physique and tendencies to flu, only to discover everyone else had some physical drawback they had to overcome, and were not the invulnerable gods and goddesses I'd imagined.

Waiting for my Italian professor, I'd hear the soaring voice of Julie Wilson, currently in a Drury Lane musical, but taking her weekly lessons to keep her voice in trim. I could only hear her if I sneaked up the stairs very quietly, for she had a superstition about nobody being made aware of any difficulties she was suffering, and would have shut up like a clam if she'd heard my footsteps on the landing. When her lesson followed mine, not a note would she utter until she'd heard the front door close behind me. I was fascinated by this diffidence from a star I'd applauded from a full house in one of the biggest theatres in London. Fancy an audience of one making her so shy!

Rex Harrison was also helped by this little professor for his spoken-rhythmic delivery of his songs for *My Fair Lady*, but I didn't see Rex at all, to my regret.

Dora Bryan was another who went there, and the professor said she was even worse than I was about her voice, so much so he'd christened her 'Little Miss Laryngitis'.

Whether or not it was this proof that I wasn't unique with my fears, or the exercises really did the trick, or I became brave enough to push all thoughts of vocal failure to the back of my mind, I don't know, but that was the end of a long spell of jitteriness, and I settled down again to enjoy my work with renewed zest. I expect I'd just been overtired.

Sandy thought we were all quite mad, to worry about a little thing like a cough or a frog in the throat which, in his opinion, was perfectly understandable and human. 'You're not machines,' he'd tell me, when he'd catch me yet again hunting for my wee box of lozenges before I left for rehearsal. 'Just you try telling that to somebody who's worked on a script for a week, and whose best joke you've just ruined by a cough or a frog in the wrong place,' I'd retort.

'Well, it's not the end of the world,' he'd say with what he thought was the voice of sweet reason.

'To an actor it is,' I'd say, 'and if we didn't feel like that we wouldn't *be* actors.'

With television, there wasn't the same concern about the voice, for there was plenty for an audience to look at without too fierce a concentration on the quality of the sound. A roll of the eyes, a turn of the head, a gesture, all underlined the joke, and the tonsils didn't become the be-all and end-all of the performance.

TV involved much more work in the way of rehearsals, of course, but it was lovely to be back for another series after our return from Glasgow, and it was especially encouraging to be welcomed back with open arms by public and critics alike. The newspapers wrote enthusiastically that we'd taken to our new medium like 'ducks to water', and felt we'd decidedly enlivened the screens and brought a welcome note of true comedy. All music to our ears!

One of the most hilarious of the TV shows for us was the episode where Bebe decided to introduce a chimp to the adventures. We didn't see the creature until dress rehearsal day in the studio, and he was an absolute darling. We all fell in love with him at first sight, and he could truly do everything but talk.

There was a phoney light switch in the hall, which one just pushed up or down according to the story, but whose light was controlled by the prop lads. I never saw anything more comical than that chimp reaching up with his long arm, flicking the switch up and down, and then gazing up in puzzlement at the bulb trying to figure out why it didn't go on and off. Apart from the comedy of the sight, I was astounded that a chimp could understand how to operate a light switch at all.

He loved hats, and sent us all into peals of laughter by constantly seizing Ben's and trying it on.

I was delighted to discover he understood every word I said. When I asked, 'Do you like it here, Johnny?' he shook his head sadly, gazing with his mournful brown eyes into mine, as though searching for sympathy. And when I said, 'Where's your hat?' he clapped his hands to his head to see if it had fallen off.

He loved my peppermints, and ate them by the packet. And because I was the smallest person in the studio, he seemed to feel he was a big tough guy beside me, and he'd seize my hand and race me round and round the set, laughing and chattering with delight. You can well imagine how this went down with the others, particularly Ben, who decided I'd found a long-lost uncle.

But the best laugh came in a scene with Ben, who had to appear in his shirt tail. The chimp gazed in wonderment at

Ben's bare legs, then decided to investigate a bit further and bent down, hand resting on the floor, and peered curiously up the shirt! The whole studio dissolved in laughter, and Ben's reactions were not repeatable!

We seemed all set for a really first-rate performance, when Johnny decided he'd had enough. He was tired, and he went into a huff. Talk about coaxing a temperamental star! It wasn't in it. He sat with his back to us. He stamped his foot. He sulked. He pursed his lips, and blew raspberries at us. He shrieked in indignation when we tried to move him. We thought we'd never get the show 'in the can', but by dint of lots of flattery and lavish peppermint bribery we finally managed it.

But not before Johnny had triumphed in the little matter of wardrobe. Bebe had dressed herself, Barbara and Doris in fur stoles for the purposes of the plot. In fact Ben at one point thought I ought to have one too, just to be upsides with the others, but Bebe felt it might not be right for Aggie to be so dressy. Well when we came to that particular scene, Johnny, who'd been co-operating pretty well after his stunts, suddenly went berserk. He shrieked, he chattered furiously, and he leaped at Bebe's fur. Bebe was sure it was just a matter of his getting used to the furs, but we all yelled at her to take it off before he tore it off. I was thankful I'd refused the offer of a fur myself! All of them had to remove their stoles before Johnny would quieten down. He gazed at me as his true friend because I hadn't been wearing one!

'There, there, Johnny,' I soothed him, 'nobody is going to wear a fur but you, pet, you've upstaged them all!' It was maybe only my imagination, but he seemed to grin, the cheeky monkey, and we got on with shooting the scene.

Animals can pose terrible problems, but Bebe adored using them in the plot, and was always happily confident that they would act as reliably as any trouper in the cast!

So, before an invited audience, for our final show of one series she decided it would be a terrific idea to introduce a pack of hounds. We were supposed to be having a cocktail party, and the set was dressed with plates of sausages, crisps, nuts, little smoked salmon sandwiches, and other delicious tit-bits, all real, for the intention was that we'd eat them at the end, washed down with champagne, as a sort of genuine farewell party to celebrate the finish of that successful series.

We'd only rehearsed with the hounds on a bare stage, for the food had to be kept fresh and attractive for the actual show.

Everything went fine at rehearsal.

But when it came to the performance which was being recorded, and the hounds should have rushed about licking our faces and then been chased round the furniture and sent leaping out of windows and through doors, they took one look at all that lovely food and ignored us. They devoured every sausage and every smoked-salmon sandwich in sight. They then went on to the crisps and nuts!

We couldn't re-shoot the scene, for we had no more food and all the shops were shut. Not only did they ruin the action, they did us out of our party, the brutes!

They wouldn't even go through the motions of pretending to be afraid of us, and far from leaping through doors and windows, they trotted quietly back to their cages at the back of the stage, full of our food, lay down peacefully, obviously happy to have a wee snooze till it was time to go home.

What could we do but laugh?

'No more animals, Bebe,' said Ben.

'All right, Daddy,' she said, 'no more animals.'

No, not till the next time, we thought!

Bebe loved introducing the old Scottish rivalries into the script, and as well as the usual Edinburgh-Glasgow feud, she included a scene in one script which had me, as Aggie MacDonald, throwing the scarf my boyfriend had given me as a Christmas present straight into the dustbin because it was a Campbell tartan.

I feared the worst from all the Campbells, but it was taken in good part, and all the letters we received were written in humorous vein. The most amusing one was from a family in Ireland who wrote to tell us that the mother had been born a Campbell and had deaved the whole family for years with her tales of the glories of her clan. After our show, the husband wrote to me and thanked me, saying that since the show his wife had been reduced to a welcome silence on the subject! And he felt sure they'd heard the last of her bragging about those damned Campbells!

One of the most vivid memories I have of the dozens of shows we did, was the night at Wembley studios when the cameras broke down. We'd moved from BBC to ITV by this time, and were still recording our shows before an audience.

I personally never liked having an audience when we were doing our TV recordings. Bebe and Ben felt they were necessary to get a good comedy reaction, but I always felt the actor was torn between over-acting to please the handful of people in the studio, at the expense of the subtleties required for the cameras and which would go out to millions later in their homes.

Bebe loved them but they were always a disappointment to her. There was so much for them to see. Cameras, technicians, scene-shifters, sound-booms. She would never understand that they were so enthralled with all this thrilling paraphernalia, that the feast to the eyes was much more important to them than the jokes in the script, and she was baffled when expected sure-fire laughs didn't come.

Never one to hesitate where the prudent might have shown more delicacy, I tried to explain my theories to her. 'You don't know what you're talking about, Aggie,' she patted my arm kindly. But I refused to be put off. 'Try one show without an audience, Bebe,' I urged, 'and see how it goes.'

Well, she agreed, but she hated the silence and lack of reaction. We always had an audience for the radio show and she simply could not see why audiences for the TV show weren't equally responsive.

So, we went back to having an audience again. Once more my theory was confirmed that the machinery held all the magic for them, and their ears stopped working. The others in the cast privately felt as I did.

In the end, the whole thing was solved honestly and simply.

We recorded without an audience. Then the video recording was shown to an invited audience at the studios, undistracted by cameras or booms, and their laughter recorded as the film was shown.

And that show, with audience reaction, was what eventually went out on the home screens.

It worked. Because we knew more or less where the laughs ought to come, we left little gaps for them, so we weren't treading on the jokes, and the show came over with genuine responsive chuckles and laughter which made it all sound warm and lively. So everybody was happy. Especially me, for never again did I have the divided loyalty to consider, of whether to please the studio audience or the larger viewing public at home.

Bebe still missed the audience, but so long as the show went out with real audience laughter at the comedy she created so brilliantly on those scripts, she was satisfied.

Well, in the episode which culminated so disastrously with broken-down cameras, Jack Buchanan was our guest star. It was to be our final show before we broke for our summer holidays and it was a lovely script. Jack hadn't been at all well during rehearsals, and although he was his usual elegant, charming self, it was obvious that his illness was exhausting him.

It was his back, he told me. It was agony. He could only sleep for an hour, and then would have to get up and have a hot bath, which would give him relief for possibly another hour. He told me he'd had an exploratory operation which had revealed nothing, but he just couldn't find a comfortable position to ease the pain, either sitting in a chair or lying in bed.

I waded in, where angels fear to tread, with all my pet cures. We always cured ourselves in Springburn, and it was a hard habit to break. I recommended a certain type of salts, absolutely guaranteed to wash away the crystals which might be causing the pain. Kaolin poultices might do the trick, if the salts failed, or there was a certain balm for applying externally which had been magic when I'd damaged my sciatic nerve once. Jack just smiled wearily and said he'd give them a try.

We spoke of Arran, and he wanted my recipe for potted herrings, and I was so pleased he retained his taste for good old Scottish dishes. It was a time of enchantment for me to be in such close working partnership with someone I'd admired all my life. I made him laugh when I told him that ever since I'd read in a magazine as a teenager that he'd said it was a sure proof of supple youthfulness if you could stand on one leg and pull a stocking on the other leg without holding on to anything, I had never once sat down for that necessary morning activity. He couldn't even remember having said it, and was a bit staggered to find his words could have made such an impact.

In this particular episode, because I was supposed to be carried away with excitement over the visit by Jack Buchanan to the house, I had abandoned my usual Aggie white apron over dark blouse and tartan skirt and was dressed up like a French maid. I thought I was no end of a mademoiselle in my pale cyclamen organdie apron with tiny frilled bib, matching huge bow perched on top of my pageboy hair-do, and flowing streamers down my back. There was not the slightest difficulty in gazing adoringly at him every time I caught his eye!

Well, at last came the evening of the recording of our show. We had been rehearsing as usual from 10 a.m. and it was now about 7.30 p.m. and the audience were assembled in the big studio, obviously happy and eager to see the show being recorded before their very eyes. Ben did his usual excellent 'warm-up' to get them into a jolly receptive mood for our offering. The clock ticked round to 8 o'clock. The countdown started, ticking off the last seconds before we went into action – and all the cameras broke down.

It was a technical hitch of gigantic proportions, it seemed.

Knowing nothing of the innards of television cameras or the intricacies of temperamental 'parts', we blithely assumed it would right itself in a very short time.

Jack Buchanan looked pale and exhausted, and went backstage to sit near the quick-change room, while Ben went out front and did a few gags to keep everybody amused.

A look towards the camera-men was met with the thumbs down sign. Bebe called out to me, 'Come on, Aggie, you can do something,' so I seized her round the waist and we went into an impromptu imitation of the Beverley Sisters, then at the height of their popularity, singing, 'Sisters, Sisters, there were never such devoted sisters.' The audience lapped this up and called for more.

So we followed this with *I belong to Glasgow*, and then checked the cameras again. Nothing doing.

The audience, by now convinced they were watching a variety show, began calling out requests. *Maybe it's because I'm a Londoner*, they yelled insistently. I found this quite hilarious. There we were, Bebe and I, one an American and the other a Scot, strolling back and forth like Flanagan and Allen singing in pseudo-cockney the much-loved wartime song, with the audience joining in as though the whole thing was part of the expected show.

When I passed the quick-change set on my way to my dressing room to powder my nose, Jack Buchanan called out to me, 'Molly, we can't go on at this time of night. It's almost ten o'clock. We've been here twelve hours. We'll be judged by the TV viewing audience on what comes out of the screen, and we'll all be exhausted.'

My heart turned over at his look of weary pallor, although his voice was gentle and his expression as kind as ever. I tried a grin, 'If you think it will be cancelled, Jack,' I said, 'you don't know the Lyons. They'll do a show if we're all here until tomorrow morning!' I knew what dedicated professionals they were, and I also knew that holiday plans would prevent any postponement of this first-class story to a later date.

Although we didn't realize it at the time, it was now or never as things turned out.

It was coming up to 10.30 p.m. The canteen was re-opened, and crates of orange juice and ginger pop were passed round the audience. Fresh sandwiches and biscuits were produced and sent round, to keep body and soul together. Women were getting distracted about trains, about baby-sitters, about their next day's commitments, but Bebe and Ben felt it was vital for the success of the performance that we kept them with us. Short of locking the doors, we became frantic wondering what else we could do to amuse them.

Community singing kept everybody happy for another half-hour, especially when they could clap and keep warm at the same time, with *Deep in the heart of Texas!* Barbara and I did a little dance. Bebe and I went out again and fooled around. Ben told more stories. Jack Buchanan remained invisible.

My Sandy came to collect me, thinking the show was over, and couldn't believe his ears when I informed him it hadn't even *started*.

It took until after midnight to get those cameras working, and it was after 1.15 a.m. when we recorded our last scene. We'd arrived at Wembley at nine o'clock the previous morning. And for all those nowadays who craik about extra money for working 'unsocial hours' and who imagine actors live the live of Reilly, this incident was regarded as an 'act of God' and the word 'overtime' wasn't even mentioned. I don't think any of us even thought of it, we were only too thankful to have completed the show.

Jack Buchanan gave me a wee 'cheeper' on each cheek, and wished me a happy holiday, for I'd told him we were going to Italy in about ten days' time for our summer break. I told him to look after that back of his, and try to get some rest, and to bully his doctor into trying something else.

We had a marvellous holiday in Italy, tiredness just dropping away under the benison of blissful sunshine and daily dips in the briny.

Coming back to Pinner on the train, Sandy opened the newspaper he'd bought in the station, the first British paper we'd seen for a fortnight. Under a headline 'Famous star of Musical Comedy dies', it said, 'Jack Buchanan, famous British star of musical comedy with Elsie Randolph in the thirties, and star of many successful films, died suddenly last night. He had been ill for a very short time. Funeral private.'

But we had done a show together only a little over three weeks ago! What could it have been? My heart felt heavy as lead, and a tear slowly ran down my cheeks. I couldn't believe it. And yet, the memory of that terrible exhaustion was very strong.

I found out later it had been cancer of the spine. The 'exploratory operation' had revealed there was no betterness for him, and so they had not told him. When I thought of my rushing in with my suggestions for salts and poultices, I felt sick. If that were all that were needed, the world would be well tomorrow.

Our *Life with the Lyons* television show was his last, and when it was shown on the screens, he had been dead for weeks.

The critics loved it, and although the supporting cast seldom had a special mention of their performances, for we were a team, and it was the stars' performances which drew the critical acclaim, this time to my particular pleasure they had found my adoration of the matinée idol worthy of approving comment. It helped to ease the pain a little to know I had been good in the only show I'd ever share with someone who had been an idol of my youth, and whom I'd admired since the first moment I'd seen him dance across a stage. I might have been crass with my home cures, but at least I hadn't let him down professionally.

But oh it was infinitely sad to realize our Lyons' nocturnal show had been his swan song.

I have only to hear *Good Night Vienna* played yet again

from the archives in illustration of his style, to see once more that elegant pale exhausted face, and the long legs stretched out in weariness as he sat beyond midnight waiting for the cameras to be repaired, so that he could record his final performance.

4

Just about this time, the BBC came up with a suggestion which was to have very far-reaching effects on my career as a writer, but which at the time appeared to be quite simple, if a little challenging.

They were aware, through my talks for them for *Woman's Hour*, that I knew something of cookery. They'd also had plenty of proof that I was capable of turning out a workman-like script on most subjects which interested me, and that I had built up a steady reputation with listeners.

So when they thought of starting a morning programme called *Shopping Flash*, they thought of me. They didn't want a domestic expert as such, they wanted an entertaining personality with acknowledged specialist interests, who would attract the audience of women waiting for *House-wives' Choice* which followed the nine o'clock news. *Shopping Flash* would precede the nine o'clock news, and it would be done live.

Their idea was that they would garner details from all the food markets throughout the country, compile a list of available commodities and the prices which would be operative over the next day or two, and get this list out to me at home, by special messenger delivery, in the early evening. The messenger would return three hours later, collect my script, take it back to Broadcasting House for checking and copying, and I would broadcast it live the following morning before the news.

This was the first time I'd ever been asked to write to such a fast deadline, or indeed to write about a subject which I wouldn't have hand-picked for myself. I had to devise a light, interesting, but factual script advising what foods were in season, which item was the best and cheapest buy, and then give a recipe which used the bargain food available that day. It had to be a recipe which would have wide appeal, be easy to follow and to take down over the air, and which would be almost foolproof.

I would be on the air twice a week, Wednesday mornings and Saturday mornings, with this programme.

It was a challenge all right, and, once under way, I felt as though I were working in a newspaper office. On the dot the uniformed messenger would arrive, drop in his list of prices and goods, and disappear. I'd curl up on the settee, read it through, pull over my shorthand notebook and get the script down. Then upstairs to my cookery notebooks, gathered over the years, right back to Grannie's recipes, and find what I hoped would be a popular one using the food in season that day when it was at its lowest possible price.

If there was nothing particularly interesting at rock-bottom prices which would have formed the basis of an attractive dish, I'd give a recipe for homemade bread, or date loaf, or an economical casserole.

I also sped round our own shops regularly to check the prices, and to see what their supplies were like. I had a very impressive demonstration of the power of radio when, after I'd been doing *Shopping Flash* for a mere month, our local shopkeepers used to ask *me* what was in the market, and what sort of prices they could safely charge! 'It would be no good me charging three oranges a shilling,' one green-grocer pointed out, 'when the ladies 'as 'eard you say they were only three for tenpence.'

There wasn't the slightest resentment on the part of the local shops over this. Indeed, they regarded me as the best public relations expert they'd ever had, and it cost them nothing. 'I knew you'd mentioned mushrooms this morning,' one of them said to me, 'I was sold out in the first hour after you'd been on.'

Another told me he had hardly put his box of grapefruit

outside to attract passing custom, when I came on the air telling the nation that in 'my' shop in Pinner grapefruit were selling at a very attractive fivepence each. 'Blimey,' said the chap, 'I was nearly knocked down in the rush. They'd gone in half an hour.'

Not only had I become the shopkeepers' PR lady, I had become the nation's cook! Mail flowed in telling me how Mrs S had won the prize at her local WI competition using my recipe for gingerbread, date loaf, marmalade, or lemon meringue pie. When I gave my bread recipe over the air, which coincidentally was included when the bakers decided on a lightning strike, the requests for copies of it ran well into four figures.

Many of the letters I received ended with the words, 'Where can I buy your cookery book?' assuming that I must have written one! This sent a little idea stirring in my mind, as I thought to myself, 'A market is here for a book which doesn't even exist. Why don't I write one?' I wouldn't honestly have thought of doing it without those listeners' letters, but I'm always open to suggestion, and the more I thought of writing a cookery book the more exciting the idea seemed.

I went to the BBC and asked them if they'd mind my writing such a book, using the recipes I'd given over the air in my Shopping Flashes. 'Not at all,' they assured me. 'They're your recipes. You have our blessing, and judging from the mailbag, you should be on to a winner.'

A writing friend, Molly Graham, who'd been on the editorial staff of some excellent women's magazines, and who'd interviewed me many times, helped me to sort out my masses of recipes into sections, and showed me how to arrange an index, and indeed generally provided a wealth of useful tips and advice. She herself was about to retire and write novels, and although she'd written cookery books and I was in a sense moving into her field, she was most generous in offering a helping hand.

She now lives in Devon with her husband, Cyril, has a magnificent garden where she grows all her own fruit and vegetables, and is a cook in the Cordon Bleu class, but still finds time to toss off the odd novel. A lass of parts is Molly Graham.

Armed with all Molly's strictures, I worked out a writing schedule, and kept rigid office hours for the three months it took me to write my book. As soon as I'd finished bed-making, house-cleaning and had my coffee, it was then regular application of the seat of the trousers to the seat of the chair, and hard at it till lunchtime.

Then came a half-hour pause for a poached egg on toast, or a ham sandwich, and it was back to the typewriter until my four o'clock 'cuppa', when I stopped for just long enough to prepare the vegetables and whatever else we were having for dinner.

At six o'clock, I knocked off for the day, came down-stairs and finished off the evening meal preparation, and put the book out of my head until the next morning.

Some of the recipes I was typing had been folded and re-folded through the years so often, that the print was either so worn that I couldn't read it or the paper had gone into holes. I was determined there would be no guesswork in my books, and that all my recipes would be well and truly tried and tested, so I'd down tools, get my apron on and make the dish, using the ¼ oz or the ¾ oz to test whether or not the quantity I used was right. Sandy was delighted with the variety of dishes this uncertainty provided, and when he'd be offered an original concoction he'd say, 'From the book?' and either smack his lips, or advise a little more or less of some ingredient which had gone into the recipe.

It seemed only fair, therefore, that the dedication (which later greatly amused the critics) read, 'To my husband's stomach, without whose co-operation this book would not have been possible'.

When at last I came to the final recipe, and completed the index, I sent the whole thing off to Collins in Glasgow, and vowed I'd never write another cookery book as long as I lived. It had been unbelievably hard, grinding work. The relief that it was at last complete was glorious, and the sense of freedom absolute bliss. To be free to write a story, a tale with meaning, as a change from lists of ingredients was a consummation devoutly to be wished, and I leaped into a frenzy of article-writing and bombarded the BBC *Roundabout* editor with them until he reeled from exhaustion just reading them! But he accepted most of them, and I had a high old time sounding forth on all sorts of current topics after the six o'clock news for months afterwards.

Having sent the manuscript off to Collins, I put the whole thing out of my mind. To me it had been the writing of it which had mattered, and I honestly felt nothing more than curiosity as to what their reactions would be. I knew as a practical cook that they were good, honest, working recipes; it was Collins' task to decide whether or not I'd compiled a good cookery book.

It seemed that I had. I had a telephone call, following a letter which said that not only was it attractive to them as a selling proposition because of my name, but that it was an excellent book in its own right. That pleased me very much. The telephone call invited me to Glasgow to discuss my suggestion for cartoon drawings instead of picture plates of perfect dishes. I always feel that for the beginner, beautiful colour plates of immaculately presented food gives an inferiority complex. If her own dishes don't turn out as the pictures look, she is discouraged. Whereas a funny little cartoon, taking the seriousness out of a necessary chore, makes everything much more light-hearted and possible, even if one hasn't previously boiled an egg.

So Eric Clarke, a brilliant *Daily Record* cartoonist who'd worked with an old Pantheon colleague of mine, Cecil Orr, was engaged to do the cartoons, and he and I had long telephone conversations, where we exchanged ideas and suggestions, and he turned up trumps with a splendid series of first-rate comedy drawings to illustrate a variety of dishes and chapter headings.

I had three little gimmicks which helped sell my book. First were the cartoons which made instant appeal. Second were little household hints at the foot of a great many pages throughout the book, after the style of the quotations to be found at the foot of pages in *Readers' Digest*. These were extremely useful and popular. Last, but not least, was the price! As I had a regular salary from my work with the Lyons, I didn't need to make my fortune from the cookbook. The fun for me would be in seeing how many copies it would sell. I wanted to spread the gospel of good wholesome cookery! So I asked the publishers to make it the modern equivalent of the paperback, but with shiny laminated covers which wouldn't get easily marked with the usual kitchen-stained fingering. This would be cheaper than a hardback, and I urged them to sell at the lowest possible figure they could quote, which turned out to be five shillings. For nearly eight hundred recipes it wasn't a bad buy. The royalties would be small, but I didn't care. I felt that even if a woman had a dozen cookery books, another one priced at five bob would be an attraction. Especially when one considered that even with a sixpenny magazine one only got three or four recipes at most. Whereas my book ran the gamut from soups right through to sweets and wines, with an invalid section thrown in, and lots of individual recipes not found in any other cook book. I tried to overcome the irritation buyers normally experienced when they thought they had bought a complete cookbook, only to try to look up some dish and find it was missing.

My hunch was right. In the ten years of its life, it sold over a hundred thousand copies and was a steady seller in all the bookshops until inflation problems made a reprint too big a problem for the publishers to solve. Some day I'll bring it out again though, for I still get letters in the same strain of those early *Shopping Flash* ladies, 'Dear Miss Weir, where can we buy your cookery book?'

The launching was a great excitement. I was Aggie the cook in *Life with the Lyons*, and here I was bringing out my own cookery book, published by a Glasgow publishing house. My mother was stunned when she went to town to find every window of Lewis's Polytechnic in Argyle Street featuring a life-size picture of me, surrounded by piles of my cookbook. Placards announced 'Molly Weir will be visiting the store on Wednesday and will be signing copies of her book for our customers.'

'My Goad,' said my mother in wonder, 'ah niver saw such a cerry-oan for a cookery book. They must have spent a fortune on thae foties.' She shook her head disapprovingly at such extravagance, 'Ah canny see hoo they can make a' that money oot o' a book that costs five shullins.'

My mother and I didn't know the numbers game, and that it's far better to sell thousands and thousands of copies of a low-priced book, than a few hundreds of a high-priced one. That book provided royalties like a dripping roast for ten solid years, and I realized I had been wise in my ignorance when I'd insisted on a low price. It was nice to know that I had actually profited by not being greedy.

They sent a huge car for me, which my mother refused to share for the trip to Lewis's for the signing. 'Naw, I'm no' comin'. I don't like crowds, and if there's naebody there I don't want to be affrontit.'

She approved my discreet dark tartan silk dress, my fur stole and my little velvet and fur tammy. 'Very lady-like,' she said, brushing the last speck of imagined dust off. 'Very nice. You're no' makin' a fool o' them onywey.'

And on the way to Lewis's, when the car was held up by traffic in Parliamentary Road, I felt a thumping on the window. There was Auntie Tassie, who'd been to Lewis's to see the windows, and who was dying to tell me there was a queue 'like an execution' waiting for me. The chauffeur was outraged at her leaping into the stationary traffic to speak to me, but I laughed. It was just like Tassie, impulsive, unpredictable in many ways, warm-hearted and enthusiastic, and quite confident nobody would knock her down while she was speaking to 'our Molly'. She wasn't in the least surprised at having almost literally bumped into me at such a moment. But I was again fascinated by the village quality of Glasgow life which made it seem utterly natural to catch sight of a particular car en route for Argyle Street, and to be on the look-out for any interesting vehicle during a stroll home from the town. Tassie's happy belief that she was bound to see me was almost the most surprising thing that happened that day.

She was right about the queues. The store was besieged in a way which would only be equalled in later years by the personal appearance of a pop singer. I sat at a table under an enormous cardboard cut-out of me as Aggie in *Life with the Lyons*, and the queue snaked right round the department, and out to the street.

The tills rang till they were red hot, I'm sure, and the manager's smile grew wider and wider. Old friends turned up, from Girl Guide days, from Sandy's Boys' Brigade days, from school, from all over Springburn, and from Orchard Park where I'd lived before I finally left for London. And there were Lyons' fans who wanted to meet Aggie, and McFlannel fans who wanted to meet Ivy McTweed, and I signed non-stop through all the laughter and the chat. There weren't many book signings in Glasgow in those days, and not many figures from the entertainment world who wrote cookbooks, so the curiosity and the novelty were guaranteed to bring out the crowds. I've had quite a few signings since then, but never one which equalled that first personal appearance at Lewis's, when teeming hundreds almost mobbed me, and I signed so many books that *Molly Weir's Recipes* had to go into reprint almost immediately.

The reporters all wanted stories, and the one which amused them most was my tale of having sent a recipe for a clootie dumpling over the Himalayas to brother Tommy and his climbing party, to celebrate a birthday during the Scottish expedition to Nepal. Having no 'cloot' they had boiled it in a pyjama jacket, where it swelled to perfect proportions and sent forth an aroma which went round the heart like 'hairy worms'!

I had assumed they'd have had the sense to slip a plate under it when they lifted it from the boiling water, and anyway there was no room on the air letter form to add that final instruction. Tommy told me later that when he'd lifted the dumpling out, the well-boiled pyjama jacket began to split, and practically threatened a dumpling avalanche! But a nimble piece of rescue work by one of the party, who hastily slid a plate under the steaming mass, saved the day. And my health was well and truly toasted after the birthday boy had cut the first slice of the first 'clootie' dumpling to be eaten high up in the thin altitudes of the Himalayas. By rights, of course, it ought to have been Grannie whom they were toasting, for it was, after all, her recipe.

The other story the reporters enjoyed, was hearing of how we were just about to leave for a holiday in Spain when the proofs of the cookbook arrived. There was a deadline to meet, and Collins were adamant that they had to have the corrected proofs back in their hands within ten days at the outside.

Well it was obvious I couldn't go through them within the twenty-four hours which were left before we were due to set off for sunny Spain, for I didn't even know how to use the printers' hieroglyphics which I'd have to insert if there were any errors.

And almost eight hundred recipes to check!

'I'll just take them with me,' I said to Sandy. 'I can correct them in Spain. They're all in my head anyway, so I don't need to take any other notes.'

Collins nearly had a fit when I told them the proofs would be coming from Spain, and if I'd known myself what a performance the posting would entail, I think I might have had second thoughts.

So, every day for the first week of our holiday saw my proofs tucked into the bag which held the bathing things, and the minute we'd had our dip, I was busy with my pencil, and my little reference book of printers' notes. Before I went to sleep at night, I did another session, and by the end of the week the job was done.

We parcelled them carefully in the brown paper and envelope we'd taken with us and took them along to the local post office. Consternation! It might have been a bomb we were sending to Scotland.

'Proofs? What were proofs?' they shouted. 'What value was it?' How did I know what value proofs were? I would have to fill in a special form, which was all printed in Spanish, of course. I couldn't understand a word of the official language. Sandy's Spanish wasn't quite up to it either.

No, they told us, we must go to the next town, where there was a large Post Office, and they would be able to deal with it. Their small Post Office could not take the responsibility for a package we could not properly describe and on which we could not place a value.

So we caught a bus to the town thirty miles away, and went through the whole business again. Any post office is a welter of red tape, but a post office in a country governed by a dictatorship is officialdom gone mad. When we'd opened up the carefully sealed parcel and shown them page by page that it contained nothing lethal, or detrimental to their Government, that it was all about food, with descriptions of how to cook it, they decided we must be crazy but they'd accept it and get it to Scotland. We tottered out exhausted, but victorious.

The Scottish recipes may have meant nothing to the Spanish, but during the two years I'd worked on *Shopping Flash* it was obvious that the old Scots recipes had a particular appeal for English listeners. We Scots had clearly established a reputation for preferring wholesomeness and solid values in everything we touched, and there was an amazing interest in quite ordinary dishes we knew from childhood.

Even the redoubtable Gilbert Harding, whom I met over the breakfast coffee and toast he consumed as he waited to take over the *Housewives' Choice* spot following the news, wanted to know *exactly* my grannie's recipe for traditional Scotch broth. He stared at me with such intense concentration as I listed the ingredients, that I felt it was more than my life was worth to have missed out a single pinch of salt!

Gilbert had rocketed to fame on the strength of his expertise and his bad temper in the TV panel game, *What's my Line*. He never suffered fools gladly, his health was not of the best, and I think he was constantly irritated by the feeling that he was wasting his life on an idiotic game when he ought to have been doing worthier things. He was actually an extremely kind man, and indeed quite a shy man, but his outbursts on television lit up the programme as no amount of gentle persuasion or studied charm could have done. People only watched eventually, to see Gilbert blow his top!

I didn't actually work with him until I was booked to take part in one episode of a series called *The A to Z of Show Business* by Alan Melville. Harding, Elizabeth Allen and I were engaged for *Q for Quizzes*, which was a take-off of the panel games. Charlie Chester was to be compère, and during our afternoon rehearsals Charlie started explaining details of some of the quiz games we'd be doing in the actual performance.

As I wasn't sure whether Charlie was just giving us a run-down of what he'd be saying later on that evening, or whether we ought to be committing these instructions to memory at once, I asked, in all innocence, 'Will you be telling us all this in front of the audience, Charlie, or should we remember them now?' Gilbert blazed out in one of his oft-seen bursts of choleric irritation, 'Oh, why do you waste time asking such questions – you won't remember any of them.'

That did it.

I was furious. I had a reputation as a panellist myself, and I didn't want to make a fool of myself. How dared Gilbert Harding call my natural desire for information 'wasting time'.

'I certainly will remember them,' I turned on him fiercely, 'I have an excellent memory, Gilbert Harding. I'm being paid to do this show, and I'm jolly sure I'm going to do it to the best of my ability.'

The studio was electrified.

Poor Gilbert stared at me, speechless.

Before he or I could draw breath to resume our battle, our producer, Bryan Sears, had dashed down from his control box. I was sure I was going to be ticked off for my cheek, but Bryan wasn't in the least angry about the clash of temperament. He was grinning from ear to ear.

'Excellent. That's the stuff, Molly!' he exclaimed delightedly. 'Don't knuckle under to him. I've got you both here to strike sparks off one another. It should make for a very lively programme.'

Gilbert and I stared at each other, then burst out laughing. His bark was far worse than his bite, and in five minutes we were chatting like old friends. Bryan told me afterwards that Gilbert had said I was a very sensible Scot. And a very conscientious one!

I grew very fond of him, although my mother never could forgive his bad temper when dealing with unfortunate contestants in the panel games, when he tore them to ribbons when they were unavoidably stupid.

Gilbert lived in Brighton, and I happened to be there on holiday one year with my mother who, I thought, deserved a look at 'London-by-the-sea' as a change from all-too-familiar Pinner. She loved everything about Brighton except Gilbert Harding, and she was outraged one morning when I read from the paper that it was his fiftieth birthday and said that I was going to hand in a bottle of wine to mark the occasion. His flat was just across the road from the one I had rented, so it was no trouble to make that small gesture to the outwardly crusty old bachelor.

'You're surely no' gaun tae gi'e that auld devil a birthday present?' my mother said. 'Ye've mair money than sense. Ye must be wrang in the mind.'

She refused to believe she might actually like him if she knew him better. Nor would she come with me when I handed in the wine.

But I knew his sense of humour, and I treasured the marvellous story he told me concerning Feliks Topolski, the artist. When all the buildings being erected for the celebration of the Festival of Britain in 1951 were nearing completion, it was suddenly realized that a large expanse of ugly brick bridging would be seen by the King when he passed in his coach or car to open the Festival. There were hurried consultations among the organizers, and it was decided to request Feliks Topolski to conceal the hideous brick by painting a huge mural. Topolski was up to the eyes in commissioned work, for he was at the height of his career, but as it was almost a Royal Command and there was a bare fortnight to do the work, he agreed.

One day, perched high on the scaffolding, he was working flat out to get the mural done as fast as possible, consistent with his own high standards of craftsmanship, when a group of workmen paused to watch him. 'Have you got a Union card?' one of them called up.

Topolski stopped and clapped his hand to his chest in a dramatic gesture. 'I am Topolski,' he shouted, 'I am an artist.'

'Don't matter wot you are, mate,' said the workman. 'You're painting on bricks, an' that makes you a painter, like me. You join a union or you don't work.'

Topolski, recognizing the British 'working' man in his most recalcitrant mood, angrily descended the scaffolding and followed the men to an office site, where he duly applied to join their union.

A few days later, as he was again working against the clock to complete his work, a group of painters came to a halt under the bridge and looked up at him.

Topolski dived into an inside pocket, withdrew his card and shouted, 'It is all right. I am a member of your union, so go away, I am busy.'

'Right, mate,' one of them called up, 'pack up your brushes. You're on strike!'

It was no thanks to them that the mural was completed on time.

But it was thanks to panel games that we got to know Franklin Engelmann so well, and it was thanks to his acquiring an enormous house close to us in Pinner, over in the Oxhey district to be precise, that we came to see a great deal of him and of his wife Tynee, and the children, and became such personal friends. I tended to keep my home life and my show-biz life quite separate, but from the word go the Engelmanns and ourselves got on like a house on fire, and Sandy and Jingle had a very lively response to one another's humour.

When they took the Oxhey house, they knew they would require about ten years, fully stretched, to get it as lovely as they felt it could look. It had been terribly neglected, and apart from the house itself there were three-and-a-half acres of grounds with dozens and dozens of spindly saplings to be cut, hedges to be cleaned, overgrown shrubs to be thinned, and outhouses to be knocked down or repaired.

All those saplings, cut branches and thinned shrubs made the most gigantic pile that first autumn, and Jingle and Tynee decided it would be a marvellous idea to celebrate the house warming with a Guy Fawkes party. With the space at their disposal, it was the perfect setting for fireworks and bonfires. There wasn't a house within a quarter of a mile from the terrace. The ground sloped away in front of the drawing room, so sparks could do no harm. It was absolutely ideal.

It was a night of sparkling stars when we arrived, about forty of us altogether, including whole families of children. There was a wonderful view over the Weald of Harrow and Jingle looked like the squire himself as he welcomed us. 'By Jings, Jingle,' I said to him, 'talk about the baronial hall! I feel I'm in one of the stately homes!'

After a warming punch, we went out on to the terrace where the men were to set off the fireworks. We'd all added our contributions to the large cardboard boxes standing ready in the porch. The children went wild with delight as Catherine wheels whirled in golden showers of sparks, but I could see that their very own hand-held sparklers gave them as much fun as anything else.

Rockets flew into the sky and lit the scene for fiery moments, set pieces hung in the air to shouts of pleasure from everyone, and then descended in a shower of stars and sparks. We must have sent pounds' worth of fireworks into the air in the first half-hour before we all moved down to the lower lawn and surrounded the bonfire. The men looked like devils as they stoked the flames. The children raced round and round, enchanted to be allowed to throw short dry branches from a safe distance to help to feed the blaze.

We were lucky to have such crisp dry weather for that lovely inaugural party, and it was a joy after all the rushing about outside to go indoors to the beautiful drawing room and enjoy the buffet supper Tynee had prepared for us. It really was a room for a party. Well, there were two rooms actually, and when I tell you that they took one hundred and seventy-six square yards of carpet to cover them, you will appreciate I do not exaggerate their size.

The forty of us could move around easily from wide windows to the ingle-nook fireplace without the least sensation of being overcrowded.

When I rejoiced in the splendour of the setting, Tynee said, 'Yes, Molly, it's lovely for a party. But there isn't a small den anywhere on this floor where I can feel cosy and snug when Franklin is away and I'm by myself, with the children upstairs in bed. That's when a little house is a real comfort.'

I'd never thought of that aspect, and when I looked at the vast windows again I could well appreciate that it would be eerie sitting alone with all that space around one, and the walls much too far away. And, after all, nobody is having parties every day in the week!

This party on Guy Fawkes night became an annual event with them, and we were blessed indeed that in all the years when the children were small we had the same crisp, sparkling weather for the fireworks and the bonfire.

I don't drink very much at any time, and I remember on one unfortunate occasion at Jingle's, I picked up the wrong glass, which must surely have contained about 80 per cent gin to a squirt of tonic. Being very thirsty from the delicious savoury food I'd eaten, I didn't notice the strength of the drink, but found myself having the greatest difficulty in speaking. It's always a sign of too much alcohol when my back teeth, top and bottom glue themselves together and refuse to part company! I noticed Sandy was looking at me with a very curious expression on his face.

When we got outside he said, 'Do you realize that for the last hour all you've contributed to the conversation has been "Really," or "Is that so?" What have you been drinking?' Sandy knew that alcohol had the peculiar effect of silencing, not cheering me!

When I protested I'd only asked for tonic water with the tiniest squirt of gin, Sandy suddenly remembered that Jingle had been pouring drinks for two of us at that moment, one for me and one for a well-known imbiber. We now both realized he'd given me the wrong drink. I don't know what the other chap thought, unless he'd drunk so much he couldn't taste his drink properly either, but he probably just grew more sober as I grew more intoxicated. It was just as well we had a mile of walking through the clear night air to restore me to a proper state of sobriety, or I'd have fallen into bed gloriously fu'. As an ex-Rechabite, I certainly kept very careless company!

Apart from the panel games on which we both worked, Jingle was also involved in a holiday programme for sound radio which necessitated his travelling to various resorts and reporting back on their possibilities, attractive or adventurous, as holiday centres. He took a tape recorder with him to record his impressions of the places as they struck him at the time, and also for the purpose of interviewing people in the resorts, and when the tapes were edited they went out as a very attractive holiday programme.

Package deal holidays were growing by leaps and bounds, and Jingle's programme was very valuable to people who'd never ventured abroad, and who wanted a bit of guidance from a reliable source which had no axes to grind. The BBC could certainly be trusted to be impartial in every sense, and the programme had a huge listening public. This, of course, was long before television sent their reporters expensively round the world!

At one of the Guy Fawkes parties, somebody asked Jingle where he was bound for next, and when he told us the next trip would include a winter sports centre, which would be reached at the end of a journey by car through Europe, I saw his eyes looking at me somewhat speculatively. The following week he rang me up at home and told me he'd suggested to his producer that it would make an interesting change to have the reactions of another radio personality, especially one who hated flying, but who, he was sure, could be persuaded to use the air ferry from Lydd to Le Touquet, if it meant motoring through Europe for the first time in her life!

All my reactions and comments, whether they be of fear or pleasure, would be taped when we reached Austria and, with a bit of luck, should add a little bit of spice to the programme

There would be no fee as far as I was concerned, but there *would* be room in the car for Sandy. Indeed transport for both of us on the outward journey from Pinner to Berwang would cost us nothing. As Sandy had only a week's holiday leave to come, and as I had to be back for the Lyons' series, we wouldn't be able to travel back with the Engelmanns, who had a fortnight at the resort, so we'd have to pay our own fares on the return journey. In the end we found the single fares cost as much, if not more, than package return fares, but by that time we'd had such a gorgeous holiday we were in no mood to quibble over mere cash! Some things can't be measured in terms of pounds, shillings and pence.

It all sounded most exciting as Jingle outlined it over the phone, although I had butterflies at the mere thought of that flight. He just laughed at me and asked why I was worrying about a wee flight from Lydd to Le Touquet where we'd never be out of sight of land. He'd have to pop back to London with the tapes for editing, and would have to fly from Austria to Heathrow and back with only a day between flights, and over snowy mountain ranges at that! So I swallowed my fears, especially as Sandy was delighted by the prospect of this unexpected holiday, and said yes, we'd love to go with them.

Jingle, as a shrewd, businesslike professional, emphasized though that if he or I got a marvellous job which was more attractive or more profitable, then the whole thing could be cancelled at a moment's notice. He could always find a substitute to take his place for the holiday trip if something better was offered to him, and *I* mustn't turn down a good job, especially when the Berwang adventure was earning me nothing at all.

Knowing Sandy, I was well aware that even if the great Korda himself had come to me on bended knee and begged me to stay in London to play leading lady in his newest film, I would never be allowed to cancel the holiday at the last minute and leave Jingle and Tynee high and dry. Actors are always prepared to cancel; other folk, and especially honourable folk like Sandy, never. Nothing short of death would persuade him to break his word, once given.

I just hoped I'd be up to the test, if it came.

It did.

Believe it or not, I received not just one, but *two* film offers, and the acceptance of either would have meant I couldn't have gone to Austria. The first was for a very good part. The second, which came on the very day we were packing in readiness to leave that night, will always remain a mystery, for, knowing that I must refuse it, I didn't want to know too much about it so that I wouldn't brood too much in the wee sma' hours. My heart was heavy as lead at having to turn down this work, for I have always loved filming, but I really had no choice, things having gone so far. Sandy would never have forgiven me. Jingle would have understood, but not Sandy.

And then, believe it or not, the whole trip was almost cancelled on the Engelmanns' part. They arrived at our door to collect us, in the cold dark of the winter evening, and Tynee was so upset she wouldn't even get out of the car or come into the house. Little Alexis, their younger daughter, had gone down the night before with what they thought might be measles. Or scarlet fever! Or any one of half a dozen childish infectious ailments. It was impossible to be accurate at this early stage.

Tynee was distracted. She wanted to stay with Alexis, and yet she didn't want to upset everyone's plans. The doctor told her to go, and Jingle was willing to accept the doctor's advice. Tynee wasn't. The doctor was reasonably sure it was nothing really serious, but he couldn't give the positive guarantee Tynee's heart demanded, for with young children one just never knew.

In the end, torn every way, she'd agreed to keep to the holiday plans.

I poured the hot tea I'd prepared for them, straight down the sink. We closed the door behind us, and set off, very silent.

Suddenly I gave a start of alarm. Had I removed the gas poker from the boiler fire? We'd stuck it in to burn up some rubbish before we left, but in all the drama of Alexis's illness, I couldn't for the life of me remember taking it out.

What should I do? A mere poker seemed a trifling worry against the brooding silence of Tynee, and yet it was our house which was at risk. Could I bowl along without saying a word, when the house could easily be burnt to the ground before we'd got even the length of Lydd!

A whole half-hour passed while I fretted and sweated. Wanting to speak, frightened to speak, frightened *not* to speak!

At last I knew I just had to speak. In a small, shaking, apologetic voice I asked if Jingle could possibly stop the car so that I could ring our neighbour, just to put my mind at rest that I hadn't left the gas poker in the fire.

Alexis's measles or fever were completely forgotten as we all competed to be first to spot a public telephone box. It was Tynee who saw it first, and in seconds I was out of the car and dialling Mrs Poupard, who always had our key, and who was extremely surprised to hear my voice when she'd said goodbye to me earlier in the day, and assumed I was now well on my way to Lydd. I told her I'd hang on till she went in to check the boiler fire, and make sure a red-hot poker wasn't rapidly melting there! She went like the wind, for the house was semi-detached and she wanted no disasters through the adjoining wall! She was back before my coins had run out. All was well. The poker was cool, sitting safely in its accustomed place, and doing nobody any harm.

But she agreed I was quite right to make assurance doubly sure, for it was no trouble to her to pop in to quieten both our minds.

This little interlude broke the tension in the car, and in the teasing which followed we were soon back to our old happy friendly relationship.

But when I went to bed that night in the hotel near Lydd, I lay awake for hours, feeling that all the omens for this dreaded flight were bad. Two film parts turned down. I felt in my bones I'd never be asked to work for either producer again – I wasn't! Tynee miserable and worried over Alexis. Jingle concerned that he'd done the right thing in going ahead with the holiday. Me so dithery that I hadn't even been sure about the safe disposal of a lethal thing like a gas poker.

Oh *why* had I agreed to fly?

Sandy was sound asleep, with nothing on his mind but happy thoughts of a winter sports holiday. He'd been sympathetically ready to do whatever was thought best for Alexis and Tynee. Now that the decision had been made to go ahead, he was as untroubled as a baby.

How I envied him.

5

Next morning after breakfast we motored the short journey from the hotel to Lydd. I grew more and more nervous by the minute, and I knew I'd just have to swallow a marzine to calm my fears. I knew they were intended for sea-sickness, but I also knew that they'd made me beautifully drowsy and serene on the two occasions I'd had to enlist their aid on journeys to the Channel Islands.

Jingle said, 'But you're never out of sight of land on this flight. I've already told you that.'

I didn't care. I was palsied with fright.

When we went out with Jingle to make sure that the car was in the correct position for loading on to the plane, I nearly had a fit when I noted all those heavy vehicles going into what looked like a vast cavern. How would it ever get off the ground? I shut my eyes and prayed.

Jingle then got busy with the tape recorder, to capture for his programme the terrifying moment when the announcer called out our names and bade us take our seats on board the aircraft. I felt as though I were walking to the guillotine, and I have no idea what I said, but I do remember thinking they might well be the last words I would ever utter on this earth. I hoped they would be worthy of the archives.

As I'd swallowed the marzine only about ten minutes before I went on to the plane, and it took about an hour to work, it wasn't doing a thing for me. The aircraft seemed bare and comfortless. My teeth chattered, either from cold or fright, but sure enough the machine got itself into the air, even with all those cars in its innards, and from the windows I *could* see both coasts. Jingle had told the truth. I began to cherish the faint hope that I might make dry land after all!

I did.

We were through the sketchy formalities and on the road to Rheims before I knew it. One of the attractions of this holiday had been the prospect of going by car through Europe. I'd eagerly anticipated driving through the streets of all the little French villages and enjoying close at hand all sorts of unexpected twists and turns in a route never seen properly from a train. Thanks, however, to my having put my trust in marzine, I couldn't keep awake. Every time Jingle turned round to point out something interesting I ought to notice for the sake of the programme, as well as for my own pleasure, I was sound asleep in the back under the rug. I'd swim up through mists of oblivion as Sandy prodded me awake, try to force my eyes open, and mumble, 'Mmmmm, *very* nice,' then like a dormouse fall instantly asleep again. Jingle couldn't believe any adult could be so pole-axed after one tiny sea-sickness pill. He said, addressing the heavens, 'It's like having one of the children in the back of the car. She won't remember a thing of this drive. She just can't seem to stay awake.' Then, turning to Sandy, he said, 'Are you sure she just took one marzine?' Sandy assured him I had. He knew how susceptible I am to any medicines, and how one such tiny pill had enabled me to stand for *hours* during a cross-channel sea journey, while all around was chaos, without a trace of discomfort.

But I was mad with myself, especially when the flight had been nothing at all. Hardly up in the air till we were down again. A bit like the fears of the dentist. The reality so much less than one dreaded. What an idiot I was to have wasted this marvellous experience of the roads of Europe because of sheer cowardice.

Sandy was enjoying every minute of the journey, and more than made up for my drowsy apparent lack of interest. Jingle's car was a big Citroën, beautifully comfortable, which intrigued us by rising up on a sort of air cushion when we started off each time, and sinking down again when we stopped to get out. We'd never experienced this before, and it made the long journey blissfully enjoyable.

By the afternoon, I'd wakened sufficiently to enjoy a wander round a little town market. I love domestic items from other countries, and I've always found the French particularly enterprising. Tynee was amused by my enthusiasm for quite simple items. Clothes pegs may not sound the most glamorous items to acquire in La Belle France, but I was riveted by the sight of pale blue 'pegs' made of strong curved metal coated in thick enamel, of excellent design, and of a quality I've certainly never come across in our own country. I immediately bought two packets, which I may say I am using to this day. Tynee bought some too, feeling they must have something special about them if I could wax so lyrical, and she later confirmed they couldn't be bettered.

We reached Nancy that night. Jingle, who'd been doing all the driving, was absolutely exhausted. Sandy and I drove very little at that time, and had no idea how tiring it could be to be at the wheel hour after hour. His eyes were dark with fatigue, but over a good dinner accompanied with excellent champagne, it was marvellous to see how quickly he revived.

We were in a first-class hotel, chosen by him, and the trimmings and trappings were in the four-star bracket. Beautiful bed linen, enormous bedrooms, and thick soft warm towels. We didn't dare ask the price, Sandy and I, but just hoped it wouldn't break the bank. As only our travel outwards was covered on this trip, the cost of meals and hotels had to be met by us. On our own we'd never have dared cross such a starry foyer, for we were used to much simpler holidays. But it was blissful to bask in the lap of luxury, however ruinous. It *was* pretty ruinous at that, but the breakfast coffee and croissants were so delicious we meekly bowed to the inevitable and paid up. It was a lovely experience of high holiday living at its best and we never forgot it.

And to top everything, a telephone call to Jingle's house had brought the glad tidings that little Alexis's temperature was back to normal! It *had* been just a little childish upset after all, and they were having a job trying to keep her in bed. When she came off the phone, Tynee's smile lit the room, and she was so glad she'd listened to commonsense and stuck to the holiday plans. So were we!

While the car was being got ready, I persuaded Tynee to come with me for a sprint round the counters of the big hardware store on the corner. I'd noticed it the night before, when we'd arrived, and it looked promising. The shop hadn't even opened its doors when we reached it. I think the assistants thought us mad, two British holidaymakers in search of domestic hardware before 9 o'clock in the morning. I was after good steak knives, with steel handles, which could be thrown into hot water without fear of damage. Tynee approved of this purchase, and we each bought half a dozen with sharp serrated edges, a detail not known in England in the ordinary store at that time. Again they've stood the test of time and are in use in our house to this day.

Whether or not it was that rich dinner at Nancy after the long drive, or some little bug which did the mischief, Jingle didn't know but he found himself in such discomfort from diarrhoea that he just had to confess to us that he was in difficulties. We had to find a chemist without delay. We stopped the car at a little shop, and while we three stayed in the car we could see Jingle through the window go through an elaborate mime, acting in vivid detail what ailed him and what he hoped the chemist might supply to effect a cure.

As we watched him, we rolled about the car, clutching our sides with hysterical laughter. It was like a Jacques Tati film. There was Jingle, tall and serious and dignified one minute, the next bent over holding his stomach, then sinking into a sitting position, writhing grimacing and twitching, then standing up, and pulling an imaginary chain. All this under the startled gaze of a thin little Frenchman, with pince-nez, who kept casting anxious glances towards the door as though making sure of an escape route if this madman suddenly became even more violent.

In despair of ever making himself understood, Jingle turned to the window and mouthed an invitation to us, amazed by the sight of us laughing, and we all joined him in the shop and began searching the shelves to see if we could find for ourselves a sure-fire cure. The Frenchman stood by helplessly, probably deciding he'd been invaded by lunatics or drug fiends, but not quite knowing what to do since he was clearly outnumbered. It was almost lunchtime and the place was deserted.

Suddenly with a cry of triumph Jingle found something which he knew would help him. Charcoal granules! The shopkeeper, almost crying with relief that his till was intact and his stocks unharmed, shovelled a reckless quantity into a jar, took the francs, and bowed us warily out of the shop, bolting the door behind us.

Once outside in the street and hanging on to the bottle like a life-saver, Jingle went through the whole pantomime again, all of us shouting with laughter, tears streaming down our cheeks as we remembered every detail, until Jingle looked down at the bottle and realized he had the blessed charcoal but no water to wash it down!

He had to have some without delay if he wasn't to do himself a mischief with all this hysterical giggling so, water or no water, he thrust a handful into his mouth and began chewing desperately, instantly transforming tongue, mouth and teeth into black horrors. We were aching with laughter as we showed him his face in the mirror, and it was a full five minutes before we had settled down calmly enough to drive away.

Only then did the little chemist consider it safe to creep out from behind the door where he'd been watching us, and scuttle home for his own lunch. We saw him through the rear window, but he didn't respond to our waves!

The neatness and tidiness of the villages we were now driving through were in dramatic contrast to those we'd left behind us in France. Even if we hadn't known we were in a different country and among a different race, the immaculate appearance of the villages would have spoken louder than the German words which we picked up on the road signs.

It grew very cold. The snow began falling when we reached Ulm, and it grew denser with every mile. The blizzard became so blinding that the windscreen wipers were powerless to keep the glass clear. Again and again Sandy had to get out of the car to clear it, so that Jingle could see where he was driving. I must say I had to admire Sandy's quiet fortitude in leaving the warmth of the car so frequently to stumble into the icy snow outside, without a murmur of complaint or suggestion that it was uncomfortable. It's one of his most admirable characteristics, that he never moans about what cannot be helped. I think he surely cut his teeth on the old Vere Foster precept, 'What can't be cured must be endured'.

The whole journey now began to take on the quality of an endless dream. We drove for hours through empty snowy countryside, climbing, ever climbing, and hardly able to see more than a few yards ahead.

Just when I suspected we might be lost, a cluster of little lights ahead revealed the Austrian frontier post. We shivered at the prospect of having to get out of the car and show our papers individually to Passport Control. We were cold and stiff and tired after a day's driving, and we just didn't want to stir. When I suggested we just hand the four passports out of the windows, I was told not to be silly, they'd want to look at all four of us under the lights and examine the passports' photographs. Brought up to believe in the legend of German efficiency and cold thoroughness, we didn't dream that the frontier officers were human like ourselves, and no keener than we were to make a lengthy job of this official chore, *or* to leave the warmth of their fire!

As though they'd heard my suggestion, they seized all four passports, and after doing no more than counting heads rushed inside the little building, applied the official stamp, and thrust them through the car window again. And we were on our way.

We reached Berwang at ten o'clock at night. We saw a handful of houses, a few hotels and a church, neatly arranged in a valley like a saucer. It looked utterly enchanting in the moonlight, and the snow had at last stopped. It was unbelievable after the endless wastes of snowy landscapes that we had actually arrived in the right place. I took off my best bonnet to Jingle for a splendid piece of navigation and driving.

We were staying at the chalet of a ski instructor recommended to Jingle, who would provide us with bed and breakfast. We would dine anywhere that took our fancy for the other meals.

We discovered it was a typical Austrian wooden chalet, smelling delightfully of wood smoke and warm timbers. Over a welcome brew of steaming hot coffee we were told by the others in the bar that there had been plenty of snow, but no sunshine at all. Sandy and I are legendary among our friends for our luck with holiday weather, so I smiled at them confidently and said with complete assurance, 'Morgen kommt die Sonne.'

And in the morning the sun did come and the others round the breakfast table decided I was a witch.

And it shone for the whole of the week.

We learned later that it stopped shining on the day we left, and never appeared again for another week.

Talk about luck! We counted our blessings and sent up a prayer of thanks for such perfect conditions.

It was a marvellous seven days. Tynee and Jingle skied on the slopes in the mornings and Sandy and I went walking. We neither of us ski, and after a traumatic experience a year or so previously when we'd been to Igls and I'd broken my nose on the ice rink, I had a deep suspicion of any sporting aids which were supposed to be of assistance to speed me through the snow and ice. I trusted only my own two feet. So we walked.

In the afternoons we all four of us went walking together,

and the Engelmanns were amazed to discover how pleasant it could be. People who go to the slopes always seem to feel they *must* be on skis all the time, and they end up seeing nothing of the surrounding villages. When one is not an expert skier, which neither Jingle nor Tynee pretended to be, it is exhausting and frustrating to toil up and down the nursery slopes all day long, and they found walking made a nice change.

Except on the day when we decided to climb a fairly steep hillside a mile or so from Berwang. Jingle was determined to bring with him a prized pair of naval binoculars which seemed to me to weigh half a stone at least! They really were abnormally heavy. When one wished to look through them, the elbows had to be leaned on something or somebody to keep the supporting hands steady. I looked at them with foreboding, for I felt we had enough to do to carry ourselves up that hill, and I knew the Engelmanns were not so used as we were to long walks or long climbs. I felt I knew who'd end up carrying those leaden-weighted glasses!

As we scrambled up the steep hillside, Jingle's shoes didn't seem adequate for the slippery conditions, and he kept slithering back half a dozen times in as many yards, the weighty binoculars swinging heavily against him as he lost balance. Sandy quietly took the straps and slipped them on to his own shoulder, and although he protested that he was fine, poor Jingle was obviously glad to be relieved of this handicap. We all made excuses for his shoes, but it was dismaying to see what a difficult challenge the hill presented to him.

When we reached the half-way resting hut, where the chairs were laid out on the terrace, his breath was rasping so nosily it was alarming. He threw himself down on a chair, gasping, and as I tried to think of something light to say to make a small joke to cover the moment, Tynee, guessing what was in my mind, shook her head almost imperceptibly. She took my arm and we moved to the edge of the terrace to look at the view. 'Don't say anything,' she murmured, 'he will be terribly embarrassed. He'll be all right in a minute. Just don't mention it.'

Sandy looked at me, and I knew he shared my feelings of guilt in appearing callously to be admiring the mountain scenery, while Jingle lay at our back gasping like a fish out of water, fighting for an easy breath.

When, many years later, my radio told me that Franklin Engelmann, better known as Jingle, had that morning dropped dead of a heart attack, that scene by the mountain hut flashed before my eyes. How could we not have realized that Jingle's heart was not a hundred per cent sound? But we had no experience in such matters and just thought he was out of condition. We had none of us recognized the shadow of future tragedy when we saw it. It was just as well we were all so ignorant, for we went on to finish the climb and nothing was said. We walked every day of the holiday, revelling in the sun, the dry crisp air, and the good company.

The morning Jingle had to fly back to London with the tapes, to complete the recording for the holiday programme, was a bit of fun. We saw him off to the local train, which he had to catch to get to the nearby airport. He presented a comical sight among all the gaudily dressed skiers. For the London trip he wore his Homburg, dark suit, and gloves, carried a briefcase, and looked every inch the perfect city businessman.

Sandy took a photograph which he captioned, 'Engelmann about to catch the 8.10 to the city'. The whole outfit looked hilariously at odds with the unsullied snow and the glittering mountain range behind him, and even now when we look at it, it still makes us laugh. But with a deep sadness too, that Jingle can no longer share the joke with us.

It seemed strange to be without him for the two days he was in London, and we were all glad to welcome him back again. He was always excellent, stimulating company.

One night after his return, as we were dressing for dinner, somebody came rushing in to the chalet and handed us a telegram. It was from the BBC, addressed to me, and they wanted to know whether or not I could take part in a TV show the following week. I had to reply to Shepherds Bush immediately, so that they could go ahead and plan the programme.

Have you ever tried dictating a wire in German from the kitchen of a ski chalet, with the family meal being prepared all round you? It was a Marx Brothers film come to life. Everybody waded in with suggestions. I speak a little German but my vocabulary wasn't really so polished that I could light-heartedly ask to be put through to International Telegram Services, and then start dictating to a German operator a message which would have to be spelt out 'H – Heinrich, S – Sonne,' at every misunderstood word.

It took half a dozen attempts just to get through to the operator. Nobody could believe in that small resort that I actually wanted International Telegram Services and I kept having to repeat that there had been no misunderstanding. Yes, I really did want that Service.

By the time I was at last connected with the right operator, the kitchen was full of helpful characters. The cook and the waiter, Sandy, and eventually Jingle and Tynee (now dressed for dinner) all waded in to lend a hand. Or rather a voice. I was in my dressing gown, my hair half up and half down just as it was when the original telegram had arrived. Sandy was still in his hill-walking clothes. We hadn't had time to complete our change to dinner-dress if the telegram were to reach the BBC in time.

While I was getting through to the correct operator, Sandy managed to find a pen to draft out my reply, so I could dictate what I wanted to say without hesitation or fumbling for the correct phrase. Mercifully, Jingle was aware of the importance of keeping faith with the BBC and waded in enthusiastically with suggestions which made sure the message would get through. A non-professional could well have been furious over all this fuss, not to mention the delay of a much-needed dinner, but Jingle understood, and so did Tynee. As for the kitchen staff, they were enthralled to be part of a drama which involved the mighty British Broadcasting Corporation, and it was all taking place under their very eyes as they seasoned soup, tested potatoes, seared meat in sizzling fat, and whipped cream to accompany the apfel strudel.

Before this interesting audience, I mouthed slowly and distinctly into the telephone, 'Telegram to BBC . . . B – Bruder, B – Bruder, C – Censur.' When I started on the actual message, everybody chipped in with the appropriate word to illustrate the letter in question, for, of course, each word had to be in German, as I was after all speaking to a German-speaking operator. 'S – Sonne,' shouted Tynee. 'U – Ulrich,' called Jingle. 'D – Dame,' cried the waiter. 'K – Kuchen,' said the cook triumphantly, associating the letter with his own domain. The next word began with F. 'F . . .' Nobody could think of an appropriate German word. Then suddenly Sandy yelled 'F – Furtwangler,' at which the entire kitchen burst into loud laughter and sent me into a fit of giggles, much to the irritation of the voice on the other end of the line.

How that telegram ever reached the BBC or made sense I'll never know, but it must have done because when I got home the confirmatory contract was waiting, and I took part in the TV show as arranged.

The most amazing thing to me about this whole episode was the fact of the BBC being able to find me in a tiny Austrian village, when I had told no one where I was. As I puzzled out how they managed it, it slowly dawned on me that they must have contacted the Lyons, who would have told them I was on holiday somewhere with Franklin Engelmann, and as he normally went abroad on behalf of the holiday programme, their office would have an overseas address for him.

I was fascinated by this piece of information, and impressed once again with this confirmation of the old truth that the moment an actor goes on holiday, everybody wants him. You can sit on your bottom for a year and nobody will look your way, but just dare to arrange a vacation and suddenly you, and you alone, are the one person who is right for a particular job. It never fails.

Every actor experiences this, which is one reason why few of them ever fix a holiday. Another experience we actors share is that of long spells of 'resting', our euphemism for unemployment, followed by a nerve-racking clashing of offers which never space themselves out, but which present you with choices you'd much prefer not to make. You want to do *all* of them, naturally, but you can't. For everything overlaps by a few days, and directors are deaf to your plea to be allowed to start a little later with rehearsals for their show. How dare you? They want all your attention, from the first second of the first rehearsal, until the show is 'in the can'. And that's that. So you are forced to reject something which, in the long empty days of 'resting' you'd have given your eye teeth to do and you spend a lot of time in the following days praying you've made the correct choice.

I've always had a great admiration for Alan Melville's writing. After doing the A–Z quiz show which he devised, I kept hoping he'd remember me for future productions, and as we all do in this mad profession where personal contact is vitally important, I dropped him little reminders from time to time to jog his writing elbow! When at last I was given a part in a TV revue he'd written, I was delighted. All those wee notes and stamps had paid off. Aye, it just showed you, it was the right thing to keep in touch. When I received the script, my enthusiasm was tempered with disappointment that the part was so tiny. Still, it was a Melville show. It would be witty, and clever, and a lot of fun.

The ink was scarcely dry on the contract I signed than I had an offer to appear in a play which was being put on specially in Edinburgh for the Royal visit of the King and Queen of Norway! What a 'heart', as Miss Chree would have said. I would have sacrificed six months' wages to be in that stage play, in Scotland's capital, on such an important occasion. But how could I go to Alan Melville, and the TV producer, after all those little reminders, and tell them I didn't want to do the show for them? It would have looked as though I was only interested in working for them if nothing better offered. And who knew, they may even have devised this little part especially to please me. I knew I could never ask them to release me.

So I did the revue. And I tried to follow Marjorie Fielding's advice and put the offer of the play out of my mind. But it was hard. Indeed it was impossible, for I have remembered it after all these years, and even at this distance in time I can feel the keen bite of my disappointment.

But after that little 'cough and spit' in the revue (the theatrical term for a few lines), I was offered a lovely demanding leading rôle in one of the episodes in the TV series *No Hiding Place*, starring Raymond Francis as the detective. This was compulsive viewing for the entire country, and its plots and performances were discussed in pubs and in shops after each weekly episode.

The German director had sent for me, and explained what he wanted. The character I was being asked to play finished up by being accused of murder, because a whole chain of events were started by her, which ended in the death of a young girl. She ran a sort of hell's kitchen, and let rooms to all sorts of dubious characters, and the director wanted someone who wouldn't arouse suspicion in the minds of the viewers, yet who could suggest by her playing a feeling of conspiracy and evil meanness which would make the ending logical. He didn't want people to say 'Ridiculous, she would never have committed a murder even by default – she's just not the type.'

He asked me if I felt I could combine this surface ordinariness with the suggestion of evil, and I said I thought I could. So I read for him, and he gave me the part. I was elated. Not only does the comic want to play Hamlet, there's a great attraction in playing a bad character when you've always been one of the goodies.

To get a completely honest reaction from everyone, I didn't say a word outside the rehearsal room about my being the murderer. Not even to Sandy. To him I just said it was a terrific part, and that I'd require his help with the words, for I hadn't learned such a long part for years. Television was all performed 'live' in those days, and I had to be word perfect.

Sandy was highly amused to be playing Raymond Francis's part, for like everybody else, he was a great fan of the famous detective, and it became a nightly hilarious performance as he donned his snap brim, and descended our stairs before plunging into his part! We could hardly get our lines out for laughing. Not exactly calculated to build up 'character', but helpful just the same with memorizing the dialogue.

I easily lulled Sandy's suspicions as to who the murderer might be, by stopping our rehearsals at home when we reached Act III. 'Oh, we won't bother about that,' I'd say, 'it's mainly concerned with the prison scenes, and I've practically no dialogue.' The director, too, helped me in this deception, for when we rehearsed he'd say, 'We'll just go to the final scene with you being accused, Molly, so you needn't hang about while we go through the prison scenes with the other prisoners.' So I was always home fairly early, and was able to say, quite truthfully, that they were doing the prison scenes where I wasn't required.

And when Sandy asked who the murderer actually was among all those red herrings, I told him I thought he'd enjoy the performance on TV much more if he didn't know, so he could do a bit of guesswork like everyone else watching the screen. Only actors can go on muttering lines practically non-stop from morning till night, and Sandy soon grew tired of listening to them, and lost all curiosity which was just what I wanted.

Raymond Francis did a show every week, but because of the problems of editing film, he spent the first two days, sometimes three, doing the outside filmed scenes for the following week's show. During his filming days, we actors in the studio rehearsed with his 'stand-in', and all the moves were plotted and rehearsed with this man, who also marked Raymond's script so he could work on it in the evenings at home.

It must have been a ghastly strain for him, but it was a nightmare for me when at last he joined us, for he delivered his lines at a completely different pace from the 'stand-in', and about ten times faster than Sandy with whom I'd gone over the lines at home. I found to my shame that when Mr Francis rattled off his dialogue at lightning speed, I couldn't remember a word of mine! It was the actor's nightmare come true, when you find yourself on stage, not knowing a single line of your speeches. I felt I was stuck there, dumb, in a play I'd never looked at before, much less memorized! I was sure Mr Francis wondered how on earth I'd ever managed to earn a living as an actress. He, I may say, was word perfect.

It took two whole days to get used to this change of pace, but the shock of the experience gave me a headache which didn't leave me until the play was finished. I seldom have headaches, and the constant ache gave me a sort of brooding edginess which was a great help with the character, so all was mixed with mercy!

I had an enormous amount of dialogue in this play, as well as a highly emotional scene at the very end. On the night of the performance, one of the nicest discoveries I made was that because I had so much to do, there simply was no time to drive myself mad by going over every line to make sure that I knew it. I had enough on my plate rushing about from one set to the next, making absolutely sure that I was in the right place at the right time; avoiding cameras as I darted across the studio, getting myself in position to race up a flight of stairs, checking that the telephone was put just where I wanted it, and seizing props as I required them.

The worst moments to endure were the few occasions when I had nothing to do, and could sit nursing my thumping head and wonder how it was all coming over at home.

Sandy told me afterwards that he kept suspecting one character after another, never for a moment dreaming I could be the murderer. Then, when the final scene was coming up, a door opened, and a pair of feet was seen moving towards the camera. He recognized those feet instantly as mine. He said his heart started to beat loudly, and then he thought, 'The wee besom. It's her! And she never let on!'

My sister-in-law in Glasgow told me it was the night for her sewing bee, which was being held that week in her house. All the girls were expected around 8 o'clock, but as they were never very punctual she switched on the TV to pass the time till they arrived. The moment she saw me on the screen, she was riveted, and then as the story grew more and more exciting she hoped nobody would arrive to interrupt her viewing. Nobody did! Not a soul turned up till after 9 o'clock, for they had all done precisely the same thing as Agnes. They'd switched on, just to check what was happening, and had been captivated. Then they'd sat down and muttered, 'Blow the sewing bee, we must see what happens. We'll go along afterwards.'

Agnes said when they did eventually arrive, the play was discussed from opening captions to the final fade out. And not a stitch was put in that night. 'It was so dramatic,' she told me, 'none of us knew you could go into hysterics like that.'

Neither did I! In fact it was almost more than I had bargained for. Normally in the Raymond Francis final confrontations, the murderer goes quietly or with sullen resignation, or anger, because he or she knows she is guilty. In my case, as I've already indicated, I was one of those people on the fringe of crime, who allowed her house to be used by dope peddlers and who did a bit of mild selling on the side. In the story, I'd arranged for some dope to be taken into a woman prisoner to keep her quiet in case, deprived of her 'fix', she'd reveal that my house was a base for trafficking. What I didn't know was that the men who took in the 'fix' substituted strychnine to silence her forever, because they wanted to make absolutely sure she wouldn't reveal information on capital crimes committed by them.

So when she was discovered dead in her cell, the men were traced back to my house, and the 'fix' traced back to me. Technically I was guilty, although I knew nothing either of the strychnine or the murder plans. Hence the shock when I was accused.

During our rehearsals, when Raymond Francis laid his hand on my shoulder and informed me of the dead girl and my guilt, I just went through the motions of registering shock, fear and collapse. The director had said, 'Don't go over the top, Molly. Save it for the performance.'

So, when the actual moment came, knowing that I would only have to do it once, I gave it the works. I let myself feel engulfed by the terror I would feel if I were accused of murder and liable to hang for it, for capital punishment was still within the law then. I let out such a cry of despair that I emptied my lungs of air. I couldn't get my breath back!

My face must have gone ashen, I think as I struggled through my sobs to get my words out, and my chest rasped with the effort of getting my breath back. Raymond bit his lip in alarm. Then his expression changed from one of dismay to compassion, because for the first time he was meeting an entirely unexpected reaction, instead of the usual 'It's a fair cop, Guv.' With infinite pity he put an arm round my shoulders and led me moaning out of the house.

It made a terrific end to the play.

But I was thankful I didn't have to do it twice, and thanked God for live television. I was utterly exhausted. One is taught not to use real emotion in such a draining way, but for once it was worth it, and there was a great sense of satisfaction in knowing I had successfully played against type.

One of the girls in the play told me that when she saw me gulping for air and crying like that, it had reminded her of a recent play she'd done from the same studios. She, too, was playing a very emotional part. She'd been down in make-up having a change made to her hair and general appearance for the next scene, and although they'd told her she had plenty of time she kept a wary eye on the monitor screen in the corner of the make-up room. It was a live show, of course, and it was going out as she watched.

Suddenly, as she watched, she saw the end of the scene just before hers coming up, and she knew it was within minutes of her entrance. And she was sitting in make-up in a basement two floors down!

She leaped from the chair, yelling, 'That's my scene coming up,' and raced up the stairs. A studio attendant barred her way at the studio door, because the red shooting light was on. 'You can't go in there, madam,' he insisted. 'They're shooting.'

Hilda stared at him wildly. She could hear her cue line coming up behind the closed door. There was no time to argue. She did the only thing possible. She burst into tears and yelled in anguish. 'I *know* they're shooting. I'm *in* it.' The man was so startled that he stood aside, and she catapulted through the door and into the scene, tears streaming down her cheeks. Fortunately, the scene was an emotionally charged one, and at rehearsal she'd regretted a total inability to shed tears to order. She had no trouble now, and the director folded her in his arms at the end of the play and said, 'I always knew you could cry if you tried!'

Wisely, she said nothing of the reason behind the tears.

The Pinner reaction to my criminal involvement in *No Hiding Place* was quite amusing. Shopkeepers would stare at me thoughtfully, and say for months afterwards, 'Mmmm, you were a bad little tinker in that TV programme, weren't you?' as though harbouring a secret conviction that I must be a bit like that myself if I could convey it so convincingly. I could see them wondering whether the comedy of Aggie or the viciousness of the dope-peddling character was the real me!

But the commercial television advertisers were in no doubt whatsoever that Aggie spelt wholesomeness, and the character could be used profitably to promote a healthy interest in a variety of good products.

I did voice-overs for tea, for icecream, for soup, and a wide selection of other foods. I appeared on TV smacking my lips over steaming baked beans, riding in a balloon and throwing down boxes of grape-nuts to surprised pedestrians; I was seen frying kippers, and spreading toast with sliced raw kippers and lemon juice as a good substitute for smoked salmon. My mother couldn't get over me being seen recommending folk to eat raw fish, but actually the finely shaved kipper with lemon juice was delicious.

Each advert just ran for a few months and then finished at the end of its useful life.

Then I had a call to go along to a very lush advertising agency in Mayfair to discuss an idea which, if successful, would use me for many months as a regular voice-over.

For some reason, I attached great importance to this appointment, possibly because I had always heard the name of this firm mentioned in hushed tones, or seen it only in the top quality glossy magazines.

So, remembering Grannie's sage advice when I was going anywhere important, to put on everything specially nice from the skin out, in case I would be run over, and so not affront my family by being discovered in a torn vest or worse, I unearthed my Ritziest suit (grey shantung) from the back of the wardrobe where it had drooped all summer waiting for just such an occasion, and pressed the dejected creases into the smoothest elegance I could achieve.

Black accessories, I decided, for Mayfair. Yes, the black straw bag I had brought back from an Italian holiday, and black lace gloves, would provide just the right contrast to my grey straw hat and matching sandals.

Remembering Grannie, I chose the underneaths with the same care, though I don't think somehow she'd have entirely approved of black lace-trimmed nylon.

My gilt chain necklace originated from Woolworths, but it matched the hoop earrings I had acquired in France. I was having a rare time to myself, dressing up as a lady, and the finished effect was quite elegant. Grannie was right when she said that being just as perfect underneath gave one a tremendous feeling of confidence, even if there was no prospect of an accident to afford modest proof that I was a lady to my skin.

I'd been given explicit directions for getting to the plushy Mayfair address, but as usual I got hopelessly lost as soon as I ventured into the maze of tiny streets behind Park Lane, and, being so near my destination, it never crossed my mind to take a taxi. Born into the tram-car age, I am not taxi-minded. I stood and looked about me. Was it left or right, here? Which direction was 'parallel with Berkeley Square'? Was I going east or west of Park Lane? Time was pressing, and I was trapped in a labyrinth of narrow streets, each of which seemed to lead into a mews. I'd love to have had the time to have explored them, for they looked fascinating, with their bright paint and attractive window boxes.

A chauffeur in immaculate uniform, carrying a gift-wrapped package, came out of a bright yellow doorway in the mews. 'Ah,' I thought, with relief, 'he'll know the address I'm looking for. Chauffeurs have to know everything.' As I approached, I saw him lay the package carefully on the back seat of a magnificent Daimler which sparkled and gleamed as if it had left the showroom an hour before.

I coughed to attract his attention. 'Excuse me,' I said, 'I'm afraid I'm lost. Could you possibly direct me to . . .' and I murmured the address. He turned round, listening attentively, then looked me up and down from the top of my new straw hat to the toe of my best sandals. His eye was far more searching, I felt sure, than that of the witness to any accident. I was glad of my new vest, which I felt sure did not escape his judgment.

My appearance must have passed some sort of test. 'If you will allow me, madam,' and he touched his cap respectfully, 'I will be happy to take you there. It's somewhat complicated and I must pass that way this morning.'

His use of the word 'madam', sounded quite different from Grannie's when she called me 'a right wee madam' when I'd been far too bossy for anyone's comfort. His 'madam' so softly uttered, transported me to the realms of a character in a Noël Coward play. I almost forgot that the whole object of this exercise was to get a job!

I tried to protest that it was much too much trouble, but he waved my protests aside, opened the door of the splendid car and handed me in. I sank back against soft upholstery, as if to the manner born, and we purred forward. Amazement and laughter struggled within me, and I had difficulty in keeping my face suitably detached and dignified to match the car.

'Aye, clothes and confidence makyth woman,' I thought to myself.

If I hadn't had a bean, and had looked worn out, I'd have had to walk every step of the way. But my well-dressed appearance and the assurance that came from knowing that every detail was as right as I could make it had impressed him and made him accept me as part of Mayfair, and a worthy occupant of his master's luxurious Daimler.

Five minutes later we bowled up to the door of the building I'd been looking for. He handed me out like a duchess. 'You are very kind,' I murmured, à la Noël Coward (he was far too grand to tip). 'Not at all.' He bowed graciously, touched his cap, and was gone.

I glanced up at the building. Not a soul to be seen. What an impression I'd have made if only the directors had been looking out of their windows. Or even a secretary. Or I'd have settled for an office boy! But nobody. Oh the pity of it. My grand arrival had gone entirely unnoticed.

But the chauffeur's respect, the Daimler, and the knowledge, as Grannie would have said, that 'if onything had happened I would be black affrontin' naebody' had done their work. I swept forward with superb confidence, and asked for the director with whom I had the appointment.

I got the job.

And that's how I became the voice behind the cartoons in the advertisement for Mother's Pride Bread. A job which lasted five happy years, and which only ended when the policy changed. We parted on the happiest terms, with a farewell lunch for Thora Hird and myself (Thora was the voice in the north of England), a huge bouquet of flowers, a red velvet-covered autographed card, and a real silver card salver which sits on our hall table. A card salver. I ask you? It must have been the Daimler which did it! For, of course, I told them how I'd arrived that first day!

6

One day the following spring, when I went downstairs to rehearse with the Lyons at the Paris, I found a wee man hanging around the landing, who blocked my way by leaning an elbow against the wall. He was short and tubby, wearing a beret at a rakish angle, and with a jolly, vaguely familiar face. We got all sorts of strange characters trying to rope us in for all sorts of unwelcome projects and I thought this was another who had slipped past the doorman.

However, I smiled politely, and he introduced himself. 'I am Gerard Hoffnung,' he said. Of course! The gorgeous eccentric whose musical cartoon festivals were a highlight of the London musical season, whose drawings were brilliant, and whose highly individual style of lecturing had been preserved on tape as an example of surrealist humour at its very best. And I'd thought he was a nut case!

He was planning what he called an 'Interplanetary Festival' for the autumn and he wanted me to take part in it. I could hardly believe my ears. Everybody who was anybody in the world of music wanted to be part of a Hoffnung Festival. How could I, with my sixpenny piano lessons, ever be of use in that highly esoteric world?

It was my voice which had ensnared him, he told me. 'It has a sort of flute-like quality,' he said, waving his hands in the air, and gazing heavenwards in dreamy appreciation, 'and as soon as I know you'll be willing to do it, I'll work out something which can display it to best advantage.'

I was enchanted.

This was something no amount of seeking could have brought to me. It was the most tremendous compliment and honour, and I couldn't wait to get home to tell Sandy, who was a great fan of Hoffnung. He had some reservations about the description of my voice as 'flute-like', though. 'Aye,' he said drily, 'he should hear you sometimes!'

'More of your cheek,' I told him, 'and you'll no' get a ticket for the Festival, so you'll no'.'

From that moment, Gerard Hoffnung seemed to be on the telephone non-stop. Sandy was as surprised and flattered as I was when the famous voice would come booming down the line, to engage in endless and fascinating discussions as to the form the Festival would follow. I began to feel I was part-consultant for the Festival, until I learned that he was a compulsive telephone user, and if he found a willing ear, this was the way he could most happily formulate his thoughts. And my ear was more than willing. I was ecstatic to be taken so fully into the plans of a genius whom I never thought in my wildest dreams I'd ever have the luck to meet.

By the end of the summer, I felt he was an old friend, although we never actually met again in the flesh until I happened to be in town one day, and caught sight of him standing in the doorway of Television House in Holborn. I was just about to set off for my summer holiday, and we were due to start the Festival rehearsals when I came back. He, too, was to have a holiday before plunging into the work of the Festival.

'See you in September,' I called out to him as we parted.

'See you in September,' his voice came soaring back, 'when we both get back from holiday.'

I turned round to wave, and that was the last time I ever saw him.

One morning, at the beach, we opened our English newspaper, and I read with a pang of anguish which pierced my heart, that Gerard Hoffnung had collapsed and died. He was only thirty-seven.

So I never had the complete pleasure of working under his personal direction for the glorious madhouse which was his Festival. But the show went on, and I was in it.

Gerard's widow, with great dignity and bravery agreed that this final Festival would be the perfect memorial to the eccentric genius who had been her husband. Plans had gone far enough for other hands to complete them, for his death had occurred within a few weeks of the start of rehearsals.

Now began for me a series of fascinating, if quite terrifying, musical rehearsals. I loved music but had little practical knowledge of reading complicated scores, and suddenly I found myself taking part in a Malcolm Arnold special composition for percussion, written for Ian Wallace and myself, and conducted by Norman del Mar.

I was the only ignoramus who nearly collapsed with fright on being handed a score which was a jigsaw puzzle of dots and lines and strange signs. For the early rehearsals, we rehearsed at Malcolm Arnold's flat, I think, and he played the piano score, while Ian and I marked our scores to time where we came in between the explosive percussion sounds. It was no good speaking to me in musical terms. I had no idea what three-and-a-half bars meant in terms of timing, or what Letter C or Letter E meant. In the end, I had Malcolm Arnold go through the whole score slowly, telling me what the various series of dots meant when translated to percussion, and I marked them in my own individual shorthand. 'Brrr-Brrr-Brrr,' I put down, followed by 'Bang-squash-wallop three times, then count to six, then Dirra-dirra-dirra, long whistle, short whistle, screech, dirra.'

Malcolm, Norman and Ian were in hysterics, and couldn't see how I'd ever follow it. It seemed so *difficult*, they said, compared with straightforward musical counting. 'Straightforward to you geniuses,' I pointed out, 'but not to a sixpenny-piano-lesson amateur like me.'

And they were amazed when, on the first run-through after my unorthodox marking of my score, I came in bang on the note with Ian Wallace. 'She was right,' they said to one another, slightly dazed. 'Her sign language works for her.' My head was reeling with concentration, but if I had done it once I could do it again.

Malcolm's score was to be the background for a dramatized rendering by Ian Wallace and myself of the old Scottish poem I'd learned at school, *Oh Young Lochinvar is come out of the West*. The comedy was to come from the unexpected use of percussion instruments, Ian's height and bulk, and my tiny build and high flute-like voice. Or so we hoped.

It was the first time I'd met Ian, and we hit it off right away. A lovely easy character, with an infectious sense of humour, who put me at my ease immediately. Indeed they all did, for I wasn't expected to be a musical boffin, and they gave me no sense of inferiority, in spite of their own musical skills, and top ranking positions in the world of music.

On the Sunday before the Festival, we rehearsed at the Morley College of Music, and the whole rota was strictly worked out, for we couldn't all be there at once. Starting from ten o'clock in the morning, choirs, bands, soloists, and orchestras presented themselves, went through their particular pieces, and went home, to make way for the next batch. I was called for 2 p.m. and the moment I appeared at the door, an official anxiously enquired, 'Are you Hepzibah Menuhin?' 'No,' I replied ruefully, 'I only wish I were.'

When she eventually turned up, I realized why we'd been confused for one another, for she was tiny like me, if a little sturdier in build. When I told her I'd been mistaken for her, she made me laugh by her frank reaction, 'Yes, nobody ever recognizes me,' she said, 'I look so undistinguished!' And then, realizing the implication of her remark, she clapped her hand over her mouth, and we both went into peals of laughter until we were 'shushed' from the rostrum. It was like being back at school again.

It was the most dream-like feeling, next day, to go into the artists' entrance at the Festival Hall. Fancy me daring to count myself on a par with such musical genius as the Menuhins, Ian Wallace, Malcolm Arnold, Norman del Mar, to name but a few. But, of course, I wasn't doing any such thing, although we all went in at that same door!

Butterflies flew around my tummy when I went to my dressing room and hung up my white silk taffeta skirt and little tartan waistcoat, the self-same waistcoat I'd made from the scrap of tartan Willie had been given to use as a duster when he was working at a factory repairing their sewing machines, and which he'd decided was far too good for such a purpose, and had brought home to me. I'd worn it at Glasgow Empire as a guest of Henry Hall, and it had brought me luck, so I hoped it would bring me luck tonight among all those distinguished names, and that I wouldn't make a fool of myself in the wrong way.

The rehearsals passed in a daze, and I only remember the novelty of strolling about the bridges outside the Festival Hall at tea-breaks, chatting and walking with Hepzibah Menuhin, hearing all about her family, and her ideals, and her hopes that Yehudi might be able to turn up for the concert. 'But will you be able to do a musical piece with him without rehearsal?' I asked, fascinated to think they were so expert that he could just turn up, stroll on to the stage where she was playing, and join in without the slightest preparation.

She couldn't understand why I should find this at all surprising. 'Of course,' she said, 'we're always doing this at home.'

'What a wonderful, wonderful, gift,' I thought, and what a background to have lived in, to be able to take such genius for granted.

How different from the life of the Weirs of Springburn!

Yet here I was, chatting away nineteen to the dozen with this little figure whose musical genius had received world acclaim, as if I was an old chum.

The only other female on the programme, apart from Hepzibah and myself, was Dame Edith Evans, who was to open the whole affair with a poem to the Festival. I saw her in the 'tunnel' where artists wait to go on, and I became so nervous when I learned I wouldn't be on for at least an hour or more, that I vanished back to my dressing room, unable to stand the strain of watching others go on and get their ordeal over in front of a theatre packed to the roof, while I still had to face my nightmare.

So, unknown to me, Dame Edith had started her poem, choked, and had had to have a glass of water brought to her before she could continue. Sandy, aware of the traumas we all went through about 'frogs' in our throats, or misplaced stress on our vocal chords, was dying a thousand deaths thinking I'd be affected by Dame Edith's experience, and be a nervous wreck imagining the same thing might easily happen to me.

Thank goodness I hadn't watched the opening. I would surely have been undone if I'd witnessed Dame Edith's discomfiture. But Sandy, of course, couldn't know this, and he only breathed easily when our piece came to a successful finish.

The whole performance was utterly different from anything I'd ever done before. For a start, the Festival Hall was fully lit, so it didn't feel like a theatre at all. We could see *faces*, instead of the usual dark void. There was also a great deal of preliminary jokery which was quite unexpected as far as I was concerned. All this plus the agony of the long, long walk out to the stage from the 'tunnel' by the side of the theatre, me prancing cheekily behind the measured walk of Ian Wallace.

Our appearance was greeted with laughter and applause. Then two men appeared, greatly to my surprise, carrying one of those long Alpenhorns between them, accompanied by two elegant red setter dogs. They proceeded to let off balloons and, worse, they blew the horn and out came a veritable storm of feathers which they chased and fired at with guns. If I'd known in advance about those feathers, I think I would really have passed out with fright, for there is nothing worse than such air-borne menaces for sabotaging the human voice box.

As it was, I gazed in alarm at Ian, and shut my mouth tightly to stop any particles floating down and coming to rest on my vocal chords. Sandy, in the audience, was suffering his own private terrors, thinking of Dame Edith's plight, and sharing my fears.

The audience were in an uproar by this time, and we stood composed and dignified (we hoped!), trying to look as if we were privy to all that was happening on the stage Finally the two men went off to a storm of applause, Norman raised his baton for the percussion piece, and we were away with *Young Lochinvar*.

It was a perfect musical example of a Hoffnung cartoon, and was greeted by the audience as such, and had an enthusiastic reception. Best of all, as far as I was concerned, was that I had come in dead on the beat every time, and hadn't let Ian or anybody down.

Gerard's widow, beautiful as well as brave, made a speech and my heart went out to her. It must have taken every bit of courage she possessed to have faced and spoken to that vast and distinguished audience, all of whom had come to honour the husband so recently lost, and whose ghostly presence was almost tangible as we carried out the programme he had so brilliantly prepared.

Every time I listen to that record of the 'Lecture' to University undergraduates, when he speaks of the difficulties experienced by a workman trying to get a hod of bricks up to the top of a building, and hear the gales of laughter of the students, and his own swooping cadences, I see as plainly as though it were yesterday his little tubby figure, beret perched jauntily atop his humorous face. I see him leaning against the door of Television House, the last sight of him I was ever to see, and I hear that unmistakable voice calling out to me over the sound of the traffic, 'See you in September, when we both get back from holiday.'

How his bonnie wife must have missed the laughter so swiftly silenced.

Ben and Bebe were very proud of my having taken part in the Festival, and they were eager to hear all about it when we travelled to Birmingham together to be guests of the HP sauce people, for whom we'd done some advertising. We saw over the factory, and watched enough bottles of the famous sauces being filled to have covered the fish and chips of the whole of Springburn for a lifetime.

There was a dance at night, for their work force, and we were guests. My most vivid memory of that occasion was looking down at my dress, and suddenly discovering I'd lost my little ladybird brooch, my lucky jewel which I'd bought at the end of *The Happiest Days of Your Life*, and which I really treasured. It was gold, with enamelled wings the exact shade of the little garden insect, and where the wings opened, was a row of tiny diamonds. I always remember Norman Shelley, the radio actor, saying when he first noticed it in my lapel, 'Diamonds in its bottom. How very opulent!'

Well, now it had vanished, in the scrum of the Paul Jones.

The moment Ben realized what had happened, he stopped the orchestra, went to the mike, and told everyone to stand still, exactly where they were, and look down at the floor. I was amazed at his co-operation and concern, for you know how he always teased me, but he realized how I felt about that little brooch which I wore at every recording. Maybe he too didn't want to risk our luck vanishing!

In two minutes flat, somebody was walking towards the mike and handing me a wee squashed ladybird. Slightly battered, but with not a diamond missing! I have it to this day, patched with a little touch of nail varnish to cover up the chip where the feet of the dancers inflicted this small injury.

We just managed to fit in the Birmingham visit before the start of our next TV series, which we were again doing for the commercial network. One of our guest stars was Sylvia Sims, who was just at the beginning of her career. She could have had a future in Hollywood, for Ben saw great possibilities for her. Not only was she lovely to look at, she was a first-rate actress, and he wanted to assist her to make the transfer to major screen productions. But Sylvia was deeply in love, and was shortly to be married, and it would have meant separation from her fiancé, for he had a career which demanded his presence in Britain. So she said 'no' to Hollywood, without apparent regret. We shared a dressing room, and we used to giggle and confide that St Michael was our patron saint, because we both bought our bras in that famous store, affectionately abbreviated to Marks and Sparks by all of us.

Sylvia at that time was extremely delicate in some ways, and given to fainting. I never saw anyone who could so gracefully sink to the ground in a dead faint in the middle of a scene. I was sure she was destined for an early grave, and dreaded opening my newspaper at the end of our show. The memory of Jack Buchanan was still very strong.

But marriage and a family seemed to change her metabolism, and she went from strength to strength in British films, and on television, and even as I write is busy on television and on radio, where I hear her regularly sounding forth on *Any Questions*. Fascinating to see this strong-minded star in her mature years, when I contrast the romantically swooning youngster of our early TV days. But Ben was dead right about her talent, which has bloomed and graced our screens through the years.

I managed to nip up to Glasgow to do another McFlannels recording between our TV recordings for the Lyons, and while I was up I popped in to see Eddie Fraser one day, as it was getting near the end of the year and I thought I might have an idea for him for the Hogmanay programme. If he liked it, it would allow me to get home to spend Hogmanay with my mother, who seemed very vulnerable these days and greatly in need of company.

Eddie was up to the eyes in scripts when I entered, and the girl was just bringing coffee. We'd known one another since the Pantheon Club days, when we'd both acted and danced together in *Desert Song*, and we could be very frank with each other. I saw how tired he was and I said, 'Eddie, can you be bothered listening to the two pieces I think might be good for your show?'

He looked at me and cocked a humorous eyebrow, 'Not really,' he said, with a half-laughing grimace. He indicated the pile of papers on his desk, 'I've all those to go through.'

As the girl laid the coffee on his desk, I said, 'Look, let's not bother with a proper studio or anything. I'll just say the pieces while you drink your coffee, and if you don't like them, at least you haven't wasted precious time.'

He cast his eyes heavenwards, 'All right,' he said, 'fair enough. But they'll have to be brilliant to stir me the way I feel today.'

I did the ghost story one first, a modest, but amusing ballad, with the sting in the tail.

He gave me a polite smile and a nod, and said, 'Mmmm, quite nice.'

'But it's the second piece I am really most interested in, Eddie,' I said. 'Effie Morrison wrote it and I think it's a classic in the Chaplinesque style of pathos and humour.'

'Go on,' he said, 'let's hear it.'

I'd been rehearsing this to my pillow for months, and as I launched tearfully into the tale of the little girl whose world comes to an end when she bursts her precious balloon, I saw his expression gradually change to rapt attention. His eyes glistened with tears, and when I'd finished, he pulled a pad towards him. 'We'll put you into Alastair McHarg's programme,' he said. 'That's earlier in the evening, but it has a huge viewing audience. We'll use both poems, so you can have two spots in the programme.'

When we checked dates, I realized that for the first time I would have to have permission to miss one Lyons' radio recording, for Hogmanay clashed with the *Life with the Lyons* date. And I knew that if the heavens fell, *that* couldn't be changed.

I hated asking off, but I did want just for once to work in Scotland on Hogmanay, and my mother would be so glad if I were north of the border at that sentimental time for all Scots. I had a premonition that we might not have the time to spend many more Hogmanays together, but I didn't realize just how few there would be.

At first Bebe didn't want to let me go. Not because she resented my asking, but because she flatteringly felt that I would be missed too much from their household on Hogmanay. Then Ben whispered to her that it would allow me to spend New Year with my mother, and Bebe gave me a long, loving look and said I could go.

Bebe had lost her own mother in February that year, and we were all at the funeral, for we all knew and loved 'Bunny' as everyone affectionately called her. Bebe adored her, and wrote a most beautiful tribute to her. I won't repeat it all, but the parts which made particular appeal to me were the words:

As twilight drew a soft curtain over the sky and stopped to wait for night – God reached down and gently gathered our Bunny to His arms like a sleeping child. For one brief moment she opened her eyes and saw what we could not see – a glimpse of where God had taken her. For Bunny was truly a child of God and she died as beautifully as she had lived, Bunny was a rare person. She walked through life with a firm step. Her road was broad and sunlit and she feared no winds that blew. She taught me to fear no man as much as myself.

Bunny had had to have a nurse night and day for the months leading up to her death, and Bebe was so moved by the kindness of one of them, 'away over and above the call of duty' as she told me, that when Bunny died she gave this nurse Bunny's mink coat and diamond ring.

'Bebe,' I said, 'what a generous gesture.'

'Well, honey,' Bebe said, 'you can't buy the sort of loving kindness that nurse showed to our darling Bunny. She made life easier for all of us, because we knew Bunny adored her company, and we could happily leave them together when we had to be away working.'

So, remembering the mother she would never see again in this world, Bebe allowed me to go north, but as things turned out, it might have been better if I hadn't had my wish to be in Scotland. Truly, one has sometimes to learn the hard way that there is only one thing worse than not getting what you want, and that's getting it.

I spent Christmas with Sandy, and travelled to Glasgow on 27 December. Sandy had to be back at work after Boxing Day and I'd left him the remains of all the Christmas goodies to tide him over the next few days.

I took up my best outfits for the Festive Season in Glasgow, plus a Dior necklace and matching earrings I'd extravagantly acquired for the recent television ball where I was selling programmes. I thought they were gorgeous, and they looked very good on the screen. There was a large square-cut 'emerald' as a centrepiece for the necklace, and strands of mixed turquoise-shaded beads threaded on gilt wire fanned out from this stone, to fasten at the back with a gold hook. The earrings each had a similar square cut 'emerald', with little curtains of the beaded turquoise hanging like tiny fringes. I was enormously proud of their opulence, and sophistication. Quite unlike me!

My brother Tommy's birthday was on 29 December, and as I wasn't rehearsing that day, I decided on impulse that my mother and I should go down with our gifts and wish him 'many happy returns'. He had a lovely little house in a village close to Loch Lomond, easily accessible from Glasgow by bus. So we rang him, and it was arranged he'd meet us at the station, and as Rhona, his wife, was on school holidays, it was no trouble to feed and look after our inner needs! Rhona taught at the local school.

We reached Balloch some time in the afternoon, and in no time we were sitting down to a cup of tea, and exchanging all our news. Tommy had been abroad on one of his climbing expeditions in the summer, and after dinner, beautifully prepared and served by Rhona, we sat down to look at an enthralling slide show of faraway mountains and dizzying climbs. My mother was just saying, 'Ah don't know hoo ye can sclim up thae hills fur a pastime,' when the telephone rang.

Rhona went to answer it.

When she came back, she looked very agitated and my heart turned over with a sick feeling of apprehension. 'What is it, Rhona?' I asked. 'Your mother's house has been burgled,' she said. 'The police want you to go back right away.'

To my everlasting shame, after the first shock of horror had subsided, the first thing I thought of was my Dior necklace. And my clothes for the TV show. What would I do if they'd been stolen? Where would I find another outfit to fit my small proportions in time for a show two days later?

And then I knew I had to break this terrible news gently enough not to frighten my mother, whom I'd have to leave as soon as the TV show was over, for I had to get back to London for my Lyons' recording the following week. And she would have to stay in the burgled house alone.

When I told her what had happened, her eyes grew wide, and fastened on mine with a strange sort of expression, which I can only describe as despairing inevitability. As though what she had long feared had come to pass.

She didn't utter a word.

Tommy got the car out, and we gathered our things together, and piled into it. It was a night of howling wind and blinding rain, and our drive through the storm had something of the quality of a nightmare. The windows steamed up, my mother tried to wipe them clear with her hankie, infuriating Tommy, but I urged him to allow her to do it, inadequate as it was, for it gave her something to do, and she felt she was helping.

It was a mercy there wasn't much traffic on the roads, for Tommy drove fast, and visibility was very poor. Every time I hear the music of *The Flying Dutchman* or *The Ride of the Valkyries*, I think of that terrible ride through the storm to Glasgow.

When we reached her flat, the first sight that met our eyes were boarded up windows, for the thieves had smashed her long bay windows, and the police had seen to it that they were boarded securely, to keep the storm out. Indeed, it was the sight of her heavy brown velour curtains blowing out into the rain which had alerted the neighbours that something was wrong.

Two policemen stood in the middle of the kitchen, looking so calming and reassuring, and asked us quietly to see if there was anything missing. My mother went through to the big room overlooking the side street, and I went into the bedroom. The Dior necklace was safe. As was my outfit for the show, and indeed nothing of mine was missing at all.

The police told me quietly that in their opinion the thieves had been disturbed by a neighbour who'd knocked at the door to see what was the matter with the curtains; that a suitcase had been lying on the table with an electric iron beside it, and that it was just as well we hadn't disturbed them by returning and letting ourselves in with our key, for the iron would undoubtedly have been used as a weapon. I shuddered at the callousness of such villains who would dare to be prepared to inflict such damage, for sheer greed.

The police had a good idea who the culprits were, young hooligans, who'd recently been released on probation, thanks to a too-soft magistrate. 'We catch them and they let them go,' they said, with some bitterness.

Tommy was helping my mother to check that nothing was missing, as far as they could see, and she seemed a bit more like herself, having ascertained that the fly-by-nights had missed her wee 'plank' of savings behind the room door.

Tommy decided, and the police agreed, that we couldn't sleep there that night. It looked so sordid with the boarded frames and jagged glass, and the police would arrange for a glazier to call in the morning to replace the glass.

So we drove all the way back to Loch Lomond again, and I'm sure my mother couldn't decide whether she was sleeping or awake. She was unnaturally quiet until we went to bed in the bunk beds Rhona had made up in their spare bedroom.

I knew I was rehearsing at the BBC next day, and I took a couple of Alka-Seltzers, my normal panacea, to help me to sleep. But they were not a bit of good that night. For my mother whispered all night, in a sort of hushed monotone, that went through my head and my heart like a buzz.

'And when we got to ma hoose,' she was whispering to no one, 'there wis two polis staunin' in the middle o' the flair. They were that nice. And they had got the windaes a' boarded up. Ah don't know where they goat a joiner at that time o' night.' There would be a short silence. 'And there wis ma electric iron sittin' in the middle o' the table. Whit wid onybody want wi' an electric iron?'

'An oor Tommy drove a' that wey, an' brought us baith back again. Whit a road, an a' that wind and rain. But ah kept his windaes clean, or he'd never have seen a haun' in front o' him.'

And so it went on, hour after hour.

I rose and asked her if she'd like an Alka-Seltzer, which she called 'a sizzler'.

'Aye, that wid be nice,' she said.

She leaned over the side of the bunk and looked at me. 'My, you're that white,' she said, 'Can you no' sleep?'

I kept thinking that if I hadn't been with her, and if the newspapers hadn't thought fit to announce the fact that I was with my mother in Glasgow for Hogmanay, while up doing a show for BBC television, burglars might not have thought it worth their while calling on her. For in other circumstances, what could they have hoped to steal from a widow who had nothing but her pension?

A great rage filled my heart that such thugs had pity neither for the old nor the widowed, and were motivated solely by greed; they were the sort who'd neither work nor want, and I despised them with all my soul.

My mother was really in a state of shock, had we but realized it, and we should have had a doctor to put her under sedation, but because of the time of the year, with Rhona and Tommy about to set off on their New Year holidays, and me about to return to London after the programme, our minds were filled with practical difficulties which had to be solved.

Rhona really needed her holiday, and it had all been arranged. We rang Willie, our other brother, but his family had their own plans which couldn't be upset. In desperation, we rang Rhona's mother, and she proved to be the ministering angel who comes to our aid, if we're lucky, when we need her most.

In spite of having her husband, son, and sister with her, she took my mother too, and made her welcome at her hearth and in her home. They made a great fuss of her, and in all the strangeness of the burglary and its aftermath, my mother was docile as a child and just did what she was told, and went where she was taken.

When I went in to rehearsal, I couldn't believe I had left London only three days before. It felt like a lifetime away. Only the tiredness, which threatened to overcome me when I sat down, showed that sleep had completely evaded me for the whole of the previous night.

Eddie Fraser was very sympathetic when I told him, and it was he who said we ought to have had sedation for my mother. But in our naïveté we thought we could manage, and we didn't like to call doctors out at New Year for something which we couldn't explain properly, like a real illness. The doctor would have understood, but how were we to know that?

And meantime, how was I to get through the show?

For not only was I doing my own two pieces, but I was dancing and singing for the finale, ending up with a wild *Stop yer ticklin' Jock*.

Where would I find the strength?

7

When I wakened up on the morning of the Alastair McHarg show, I felt unnaturally calm, as though there was a great damped-down storm biding its time, and I knew I was in for a sleepless spell when all this was safely behind me.

'Dear God, just give me the strength to get through the show successfully,' I prayed, 'and we can worry about the rest later.'

I travelled from Balloch in the morning, having collected my clothes for the show on the night of the burglary. When I reached the BBC, I found Eddie having a quiet laugh. A telegram had arrived from Ben Lyon, the longest telegram anybody had seen. It read, 'Absolutely marvellous being without Aggie. It's so peaceful here during rehearsals without her talking. The silence is so blissful that we think it might be a good idea if you keep her up there. Or at least you can borrow her any time you like'. It was signed, Ben.

That set us off on a more light-hearted note, and there was so much to do during the day with cameras, lighting, dancing rehearsal, music calls, make-up, and the thousand and one details which go into any TV production, that there just wasn't time to spare for personal or private griefs.

And when it came to my 'Balloon' number, like all actors who can use personal experience to add an extra dimension to their understanding, I poured all my present hurt, and sorrow for my mother's condition, into my interpretation, and I let the heartbreak find full expression and allowed the tears to overflow as I whispered the last verse.

There was absolute silence in the studio, and I knew that God heard my prayer and had helped me to do my very best.

A technical chap came over to me later and said, 'I was watching you on the monitor in the next studio, and I was glad I was alone. How could a story about a wee girl and a balloon move a hard case like me to tears? I'd never have believed it.'

Another friend rang up and said, 'It was worth bringing you all the way from London just for that wee poem. Chaplin couldnae have done it better.'

Sweet words to hear.

But an English friend decided the high spot was the romp with *Stop yer ticklin' Jock* which he was hearing for the first time, and he thought our dancing and our hooching terrific.

But my mother, still in this strange mood of not quite comprehending her own shock, or my worry over her, just said, 'My, it wis awfu' sad. You had us a' greetin'.' She hadn't cried, but apparently everybody else had, for they had understood what I was expressing.

She was still with Mrs Dickson, Rhona's mother, when I left for London, and showed no sign of wondering when she ought to go back to her own flat.

In spite of Ben's telegram, somebody in the Lyons' family wanted reassurance that I was still as talkative as ever, and that I had returned, for one night when I went to the door, there was Richard on the doorstep.

'It was terrible without you,' he said. 'There were no arguments or anything at rehearsals. We just went through the script as it was written, without a single argument about changes!'

Richard always enjoyed my challenges about 'we wouldn't say it like that in Scotland', and the endless discussions which then took place as to how we ought to change the script.

When I went back to the show the following week, Bebe told me that it had been the first script they'd written which was said word for word, as it had been typed! I hoped the writers weren't sorry to see me back!

We did only a few weeks' radio per year nowadays, before

going on to the next TV series, and were working practically non-stop, for each TV show involved ten days' rehearsals. There was a flu epidemic that winter, and for the first time in his life, our Ben went down with it. He managed to totter out of his bed for the rehearsals for the first TV show, and was weak as a kitten. He was amazed at this loss of strength, and came over to me and said, 'I can't understand it, I've been in bed for over a week, and yet all I want to do is sleep. I've got no energy at all, and Bebe has just given me a small part this week, till I feel better, but I'm exhausted.'

'But, Ben,' I said. 'Your body has been fighting infection and high temperature, and your fighter bugs are whacked. It's this enervating feeling and lack of strength which is the hardest thing to endure after flu or any sort of high temperature illness.'

He'd never been ill in his life, he told me.

'Well, you've been darn lucky,' I said, 'for I've had flu practically every winter.'

Ben's strangest and nicest reaction to this illness was a new understanding of other people's weaknesses. He'd never realized how debilitating infection could be, and after that flu bout he never again went mad if anybody coughed or had to clear the throat because of a cold.

Another reaction was his bewildered realization that it was far more nerve-racking to have a small part than to be occupied with such a huge part that it excluded the possibility of a too worrying concentration on a very few lines.

He came over to me during the recording and said, 'I've got nothing to do in this show and I'm nervous as a cat.' 'Now you know how I feel every week,' I said. What a cheek I had, but at least it made him laugh.

Altogether he was much gentler after this illness, and when his birthday came round in February, he told me of a very touching incident which moved him very much.

They'd had a lovely birthday dinner, with all the family and friends calling to drink his health, and the house was a picture with masses of beautiful flowers filling the vases at every window, spotlights picking out their treasured paintings, and candles glowing on the table.

They were just settling down to an evening of cards, when he decided to put the car away before the threatened snow came on. Ben was always very set in his habits, with a keen eye for detail, and as he put the car into gear he noticed that the rug which normally lay along the top of the back seat now lay along the seat. There was something slightly disturbing about its appearance. It looked solid, somehow. He put on the hand brake again, leaned over and felt the rug.

There was a body underneath.

He broke into a sweat, he told me, and his instant thought was, 'My God, somebody has committed a murder and dumped the body in my car.'

Pushing aside his fear, he threw back the rug in one violent movement. Underneath, curled up stiffly, was a tramp. A tattered, indescribably shabby suit covered his thin body, gaping boots pressed against the side of the car for warmth, a stubble of sandy hair showed on his chin, and his thin, veined hands rested under his cheek.

One eye slowly opened, drowsily.

'Thank heaven, he is alive,' Ben thought.

Then, relief making him furious, he leaped out of the driving seat and threw the back door open, shouting, 'What the hell do you mean by it? Get out. At once!'

He told me he stood close to the car, ready to take the initiative in case he was going to have any trouble, but the tramp was too bewildered by the sudden awakening to have any thoughts of violence.

Gathering his stiff limbs into unwilling movement, he'd swayed and lurched out through the car door, mumbling, 'Sorry, Guv'nor – I just crep' in here for a bit of a warm,' then he turned dejectedly and shuffled down the mews, shivering against the piercing wind which must have gone through his pitiful rags like a knife.

Ben went into the car again and turned into the mews towards his garage, the figure of the tramp just ahead of him. Suddenly, his fear and his anger melted in a terrible awareness of their contrasting circumstances. Here he was, celebrating his birthday. Happy. Successful. He'd had a dinner lavish enough to have pleased a gourmet. A blazing fire had thrown out so much heat, they'd all had to push their chairs back. His gifts covered the sideboard. His family and friends surrounded him.

And here was this poor fellow-creature, alone, friendless, his only refuge against the bitter night a stolen rest in an unlocked car. He'd been willing to risk arrest and maybe even imprisonment for a few minutes' refuge from cold and weariness.

Ben stopped the car, felt in his pocket, took out a pound and walked over to the tramp. 'Here,' he said gently. 'Go and get yourself a square meal. Not just a drink, mind, a good meal.'

The tramp had stared at the money in disbelief, then raised his eyes to Ben, and his look changed from despair to bewilderment, and then to a dazed happiness.

'God bless you, Guv'nor,' he had whispered when he could find his voice. 'I'll do as you say. I'll get meself a decent meal. God bless you.'

Ben didn't tell me this story to illustrate what a good guy he was. He'd told me because he'd been ashamed of his anger, and because he felt a need to tell somebody as sentimental as he knew I was, of his sudden awareness in himself of a deep sense of pity for all lonely mankind.

And I had a feeling that the blessings of a grateful down-and-out had somehow proved the richest gift he had had that day.

I had my own dose of flu shortly after this, but luckily it didn't last too long, and we were all hoping for a hot sunny summer to build us up for the next season's work, and help us recuperate from all the colds and sneezes of the past winter

But it was a very poor summer, with a little hot sunshine interspersed with more rain than I'd ever seen in the London area. My mother was having her month with us, as usual, and I'd arranged that she came a little earlier, for I'd been asked to go to Glasgow to open a big fête for a children's charity, and I'd bring her back with me. She'd enjoy the journey with me better than travelling down alone later.

After the burglary, Tommy and Rhona had worked wonders and had managed to find a cosy little single-end in Springburn, not far from her old place, but one stair up, near the shops, and with all her old friends and neighbours not far away. They knew she could never settle again in the big flat which had been the scene of the burglary, but it was a nightmare trying to get her to accept that she simply couldn't take her old furniture with her.

I went up once or twice to see her on quick visits, and I drew sheet after sheet of wall measurements, showing her that it would only be possible to take her very best small pieces with her. She loved furniture, and she couldn't bear the thought that her big sideboard would have to go. In the end, Tommy told me they'd only managed to get ten shillings for it! A thing of such beauty, pale fine golden oak, with carved doors and drawers, which would have held a flitting at a pinch. It really would have been more prudent to have cut it up for firewood. But that would have seemed like sacrilege.

They had to have a new cooker, a small one, for this modest apartment, and the others persuaded Tommy that it was better to stick to gas, for she knew how to use that, and might have burned herself against unfamiliar electric plates, not realizing they still retained their heat long after their colour had dimmed to an innocent-looking black.

They also managed to install a new sink, the first brand-new sink my mother had ever had in all her life, and it was that more than anything which persuaded her to agree to part with her larger pieces of furniture and keep only what would fit these small premises. One sight of that sink, gleaming and unused, which had never known the grease of a single dirty dish or pot, had silenced every objection.

I pointed out the advantages of a smaller place, and of the

'posh' look she could achieve by retaining only her finest pieces of furniture. Out came my paper and pen again, and I drew in her small chest of drawers, with the little Queen Anne mahogany mirror with the tiny drawers sitting on top. Her semi-circular table against the opposite wall. Her brass-top table in front of the fire. The best rug in place, under her small easy chair. The small settee along the wall. She grew quite excited, realizing for the first time, I think, that she'd be sitting among her nicest things every day, for this one room was parlour, kitchen, dining room, and bedroom combined, easily cleaned, and with one tall large window overlooking the street. She gazed in perplexity at my drawings, something puzzling her. 'But where's ma sideboard?' she asked. My heart sank. I thought she'd understood. 'Mother,' I said, 'if you bring that sideboard, then you'll have to part with your settee and your chest of drawers, and the Queen Anne mirror. Would you rather do that?'

Her lip stuck out mutinously. She wanted to keep them all. Oh, how well I understood, for I am the world's worst magpie, and hate parting with anything which is tied to me with memories of the hard savings which went into acquiring it. But I had to harden my heart, or we would never get her moved. 'All right,' I said, 'we'll just tell the factor you don't want the wee flat. He'll have no trouble in letting it, especially now that it has such a lovely new sink.'

She bit her lip, and I hated myself. Then she brightened. 'All right,' she said, 'we'll juist take the good bits, juist as ye say, but we'll bring the sideboard tae and if it disnae fit, then we'll pit it oot.'

'Mother,' I said, 'you're a coughdrop. And an impossible coughdrop at that!' But I couldn't help laughing.

I told Tommy not to let her see the sideboard anywhere near the new small premises or they'd have to climb over it for the rest of their lives, for she'd never get rid of it once she saw it there, and I gave him a list of the good items I'd sketched and which would fit happily into the single room in the tenement which would be my mother's future home.

I had to miss the 'flitting' because I still had the Lyons' series to finish, but when I went north again to open the Children's Fête in aid of a Glasgow charity, she was safely installed, and so enthralled with the elegance of her new setting she seemed to have forgotten she was to come back with me to spend a holiday in Pinner. I was a little surprised, for in the past she had always kept asking if it wasn't time for her visit, and indeed the holiday grew earlier and earlier each year, just to make the break something to look forward to during the darkest days of winter. Sometimes indeed it was so early that I went up again in late summer and had another little break with her in Scotland before the dark nights set in.

Now she seemed to have forgotten. I was quite taken aback.

She had had the time of her life, it seemed, chasing round her old haunts acquiring all the trimmings for the new flat. It was a happy return to the old tenement life-style, with the double bed set into the big alcove behind the kitchen door, where she was able to take in all her possessions in a single glance. She'd bought a gold bed-cover and eiderdown, and had put up long gold curtains which screened the bed in the day-time, and which she looped back at night. The trolley stood nearby, with teapot, cup and saucer in position, so she could have a cup of tea in bed any time she liked.

She showed me how the new cooker worked, and that it was so up to date she had to press in the taps before they would light. Every night, for the few nights I stayed with her before we travelled south together, she'd say to me before I went to bed, 'Are a' the gases off? Ah'm awfu' feart o' gas.' And I would show her all the taps positioned at the same safe angle before I put out the light.

One day when we were in town for the coffee and meringues which she loved, I saw there was an art exhibition at the McLellan Galleries and I took her to this, as the general theme was Glasgow and its architecture, and I felt she might enjoy it. She was stunned to find that practically every picture was of dirty old tenements, and not the waterfalls, or the trees, or the flowers she'd expected. 'Fancy chairgin' folk for things like that!' she said. 'Hoo much is that, did ye say?' When I told her that the painting which attracted me was £75, she had to sit down on the bench to recover from the shock.

'Don't tell me you're thinkin' o' spendin' a fortune on that?' she gasped. I wasn't, but nothing would convince her otherwise, because I had spent so long looking at it.

Later, in Pinner, she told Sandy, 'If ah hidnae been wi' her, she'd have bought that rotten picture o' a dirty auld tenement, Sandy, wi' a cat sittin' in the back court wi' skelley eyes.'

When Sandy laughed, she said, 'It's nothing tae laugh it. It was seventy-five pounds, and if it hidnae been fur me, she'd have brought it doon wi' her.'

That took the smile off Sandy's face all right! Clearly he believed my mother, and not my assurance that I had had no intention of making such a purchase.

But in spite of such crisp attacks on my commonsense, which were so much in character, my mother's behaviour was strangely contradictory, and almost impossible to convey to anyone, unless one were there actually to see it.

When we'd arrived in our house in Pinner, as soon as we'd unpacked, and had a cup of tea, I'd taken the deck chairs out into the garden and encouraged her to have a little sleep to recover from the journey. I lay back and closed my eyes, to pretend I too was sleeping, for I felt she needed the rest.

Suddenly I heard her voice, and through my half-closed lids I watched her lean forward, and put out a hand as if to restrain somebody. She was half-laughing as she spoke. 'No, son, we don't need any bread today. You'll have to take it back.'

Was she dreaming, I wondered? But my heart was lurching in a most uncomfortable fear. I fully opened my eyes and gave a feigned yawn, so that she would catch sight of me.

She was still laughing. 'Do you see that wee boy?' she

said. 'He came through the french window and he thinks we need bread.' And she turned from me again and addressed a child that only she could see. 'Take it back and come back the morn, son,' she said, 'and we'll see if we need onything.'

Then she leaned back in the deck chair and fell asleep.

When I tried to tell Sandy later that evening, he pooh-poohed my fears. 'Och, she's been half dreaming,' he said, 'or *you've* been dreaming. It's been the journey to London. You know you've never been able to get a decent sleep on a train sleeper.'

But the next day, when we were having our high tea, which we always preferred on Saturdays to having dinner, and my mother was eating plaice fillet while we were eating the shell-fish she wouldn't touch, she turned to Sandy and said, 'That's the sort of stuff you'd get in oor Molly's house. Ah can niver understaun' how she can eat it.' Sandy's knife stopped in mid-air, and he stared across at me. Gently, so as not to frighten her, I touched her hand and said, 'Mother, who do you think I am?' She turned and stared at me as if I were a stranger who had rudely interrupted a private conversation. There was no light of recognition in her eyes. I felt gripped by a sickening apprehension.

She turned back to Sandy and repeated, 'Aye, you'd get a' that sort o' stuff in oor Molly's hoose. Winkles, an' crabs, and prawns. Ah could niver eat it masel'.'

I touched her hand gently again, and this time she turned and said, completely normally, 'This is a lovely bit o' plaice, would ye no' rether hiv it than thae shrimps?'

We didn't know what was happening, nor how to cope with it.

During the night, I heard movement in the bedroom, then drawers opening and shutting, and a low murmur of conversation. I was wide awake in an instant. What was she doing? It was three o'clock in the morning. I went to the door and quietly opened it, and my mother turned with a radiant smile, after a guilty jump, and said, 'Oh, hullo, I was just looking for a hankie.'

I went back to bed and lay awake most of the rest of the

night, thinking. I felt sick with worry. I began to suspect that the shadows of that burglary were lengthening across our lives, and that my mother had been so affected that she would never be the same. I felt sure she'd been going through all the drawers checking that everything was safe, and that a strange mental confusion afflicted her in lightning flashes, so that at that particular moment she was unable to identify or remember people or things. Which was why she hadn't recognized me at our own table.

That holiday was a nightmare.

My mother would hide my keys just when I was about to go out, and I wouldn't know where to begin to look for them. She'd forgotten where she'd 'planked' them and it would be a case of trying to read her mind, and searching all the likely and unlikely places.

The electric iron vanished, and turned up in the cupboard under the stairs.

She wanted to be helpful, so I asked her one day to go down to the shops five minutes along the road, to buy a loaf and some rolls, just to make her feel that I would have been lost without her willing assistance. When she hadn't returned an hour later, I was in a ferment, like a mother whose child has vanished. How quickly are the rôles of parent and child reversed, when age strikes in this sudden and frightening fashion.

I ran down the road and went into every shop, breathlessly asking if they'd seen my mother. Not one had. Where could she have gone? Surely not all the way to the village, which was a full mile from the house. Not when she knew I had been preparing our lunch when she left.

And which way would she have gone? Through the park, or along the road? I might miss her if I went through the park. But I'd have to look through the park gates first, in case she was on her way back.

I tore round to the side entrance of the little park and gazed across the lawns, but there was no sign of anyone at all, for it was lunch-time and everyone had gone home to eat. I raced back again and hared along the road, distraught, feeling half mad myself, and praying I would see no crowd gathered round a figure on the ground. Anxiety feeds upon itself, and I was sure by this time she'd collapsed or forgotten where she was, and had been taken either to the hospital or the police station.

When I reached Pinner village, I found her sitting serenely on a seat in the little garden opposite Woolworths, gazing contentedly about her, having completely forgotten I was waiting for her at home to give her lunch.

'Hiv ye been runnin'?' she said, looking at my perspiring face. 'My, the shops are awfu' faur away,' and before I could get my breath she added, 'and there's nae icecream in Woolworths noo.'

I didn't know whether to laugh or cry.

I took the last remark first, crossed the road to Woolworths and bought her an icecream, which she loved, and took it back to her. She was delighted, and together we strolled quietly back to the house, and I showed her the little shops nearby where they sold bread and to which I'd meant her to go. 'Fancy, an' I never even saw them when I was gaun up the road,' she said, quite undisturbed. 'Whit ur we hivin' fur oor dinner?'

When I had to go to rehearsal one day, I asked my dear neighbour, Mrs Poupard, to take her for a walk, and I gave her money so that they could have tea out, a treat they both enjoyed. Mrs Poupard knew my mother very well, from previous holidays, and when I saw her privately next day to thank her for stepping into the breach, she told me that my mother had spoken very oddly at times. That she had confided to Mrs Poupard that 'a strange woman' had come and taken her on a train to a strange house, and she didn't know if she was ever going to be allowed to go home again.

Merciful God, to be described by my own mother as 'a strange woman'! What was happening to her? Yet between such spells she was perfectly normal, her old self.

'Funnily enough,' said Mrs Poupard, 'she knows Sandy all right.'

And then I had a summons to go down to Southampton

again, to do another lunchtime show with Jim Dale. 'Go,' said Sandy, 'it will do you good to get away for a night and it will maybe do your mother good too to feel she is responsible for the house and the cooking again.'

I showed her the pots for the potatoes and the mince, choosing the simplest diet possible, one well within her scope, and I showed her the gases to light at six o'clock so everything would be ready when Sandy got home from the office. It was summertime and the trains were running to time, and one could practically put the kettle on for his arrival.

When I got back from Southampton, Sandy told me that when he'd come into the house the place was filled with gas, for my mother had simply turned on every tap on the cooker, including the oven tap, but had only applied a light to the top jets. So gas had been pouring into the oven from six o'clock until he arrived in the house just after six-thirty. 'Goodness knows what would have happened if I'd been kept late,' Sandy said. We both shuddered.

'But where was she?' I said. 'She has a terribly keen sense of smell.'

'Sitting at the open french windows reading,' said Sandy.

So of course she hadn't smelt the gas filling the kitchen next door.

When the rain poured down I brought my typewriter into the dining room, and wrote there while my mother read, or gazed into the garden, and we drank endless cups of tea and talked. She was amazed at the amount of writing I had to do, but enjoyed the fact that we were both in the same room, while expressing her disillusionment that London's weather could be just as bad as Glasgow's.

When the weather was fine, I took her for car runs out into the country, where she could indulge her passion for cream teas, and I bought her her once-a-year pair of summer shoes so that her feet would be perfectly comfortable. She'd never allow herself to spend hard-won cash on such seasonal items, and felt it a rare indulgence to allow me to do so. Mrs Poupard used to say, 'My word, I wish I had a daughter to look after my feet!' which greatly amused my mother.

At weekends we took her to Regent's Park to see the roses, and along the Mall to see Buckingham Palace, and we even managed to get seats for the ballet so that she could enjoy the grace and beauty of Margot Fonteyn. My mother loved dancing in all its forms.

When she'd fall into a little doze in her chair, I examined her face for signs of stress or strain. There was none. Just a serenity of expression I'd never seen her wear, as though all passion were spent. 'That is how she'll look when she is dead,' I thought, 'and how will I bear it?'

On this holiday, for the first time, she grew homesick and wanted to go back to 'her wee hoose'. 'We'll juist go up and see it,' she'd plead, 'and we'll come straight doon again.'

'But Mother,' I'd say, 'we can't go up and down to London just like that. It's too far. And it's too expensive. Are you not enjoying yourself?'

'Oh aye,' she'd assure me, 'it's juist that I'd like to see ma ain wee hoose.'

On the last night of the holiday, I ran a bath for her at bedtime, instead of the morning one she usually had during her stay. When I went up to see if she was all right, I found her sitting in the bath with all her underclothes on, plus her pyjamas which she'd washed, and which were also soaking wet. 'I juist washed everything,' she said cheerfully, 'so they'd a' be clean for me goin' hame.'

I forced my tears back, and took the wet clothes from her, gave her one of my nighties, and tucked her up in bed with a hot milky drink, and told her we were going home in the morning, and I'd bring her breakfast early.

'Something will have to be done,' I said to Sandy. 'I'll go and see her doctor when I go home with her and see what he can suggest.'

We knew it was no good bringing her to us in Pinner on a permanent basis, for she knew nobody except Mrs Poupard, and when my regular work started I would be out daily. She found the English accent difficult to understand, and with her deafness she wasn't the easiest companion to push on to strangers. And she loved her own friends and neighbours in Glasgow.

Sandy saw us off, and we agreed I should stay with my mother until I found some sort of solution to our difficulties.

When we reached her 'wee hoose', she threw herself on the bed, kicked her legs in the air like a young colt, and sang at the top of her voice, a daft childhood ditty which always made me laugh.

> *'Ah wish ma maw wis here,*
> *Ah wish ma maw wis here,*
> *It's an awfu' thing tae dee alane,*
> *Ah wish ma maw wis here.'*

While I put the kettle on and started unpacking, she ran round the place, touching everything, like a child home from school making sure all her treasures were solid and safe. 'Oh ma wee table,' she exulted, 'doesn't it look lovely wi' the sun shining on it,' and, 'you're gaun tae get that wee Queen Anne mirror when I'm away. Somebody else asked me for it and I said no, it's for oor Molly.'

My mother loved me to admire her taste, and she'd been delighted when I'd told her that her mirror bargain was a true antique. Which it was.

'And ah'm gaun tae gi'e ye the crystal vase like a thistle tae take back wi' ye to London,' she said, 'fur it'll only get broken here, and you've aye liked it.'

'Oh come on and have your tea,' I said, 'and stop giving away all your things. I like to see them here when I come to visit you, I don't want to take them away with me.'

I had of course to sleep on the settee, for she had only one room, and Sandy had told me that if my slumbers were disturbed too drastically, I wasn't to stay, but to come home at once. But I knew I could stick it for four or five days, to try to get things settled, for I had no immediate work on hand and didn't need to conserve my strength for any employer.

That night I dozed uneasily, and came to full wakefulness

to see her standing at the window crying, 'Oh a' the buildings have disappeared, and the hoose is flooded. Where are a' the hooses?'

I led her back to bed and tucked her in.

I would see the doctor in the morning.

Next day, I visited Dr Bissett in his lovely house on Balgray Hill, one of those designed by the great Rennie Mackintosh, and later demolished with the other seven by the City Fathers, who were as ignorant as we were of their irreplaceable and unique beauty. We at least recognized their quality, tenement-reared as we were, but those who were paid to serve our physical needs in the Corporation, preferred high-rise flats, to their everlasting shame.

Dr Bissett listened sympathetically and with infinite understanding to my description of my mother's condition. He had helped bring me into the world and knew the family well. He was a Highlander, well over six foot tall, and had attended Grannie in her last illness. Those were the days of the true family doctor, and I had come a long way in confidence from the days when I'd had to stay off school to open the door to him when he visited Grannie, to reach this moment when I could speak to him as a friend and seek his help in finding an answer.

'Och, your mother is a fine wee woman,' he said. 'She brought you all up single-handed, and a damned fine job she made of it.'

He agreed a move to Pinner was no solution, for she loved Springburn and Glasgow, and it was no time of life to move to an alien environment.

I wondered if there was any sort of boarding house cum nursing home where I could install her. Without the stigma attached to an old folks' home, which she'd hate, but somewhere I could feel she was being looked after and was safe. I said I felt it really wasn't safe to leave her alone.

When I described her irrational behaviour, kind Dr Bissett explained that the shock of the burglary had no doubt accelerated her condition, and that the arteries to the brain were narrowing. When the blood couldn't get through for a moment, the brain zoomed in on any period of her past life, which is why at times she hadn't recognized me. She'd simply gone back to a time when I hadn't existed. Then when the blood seeped through the narrowed artery, the brain was stimulated again, and she was herself. It made for bearable comfort to have this explanation, and it also made sense.

Dr Bissett stared into the fire as we wondered what we should do. 'Och well,' he said at last, 'sometimes I wonder if it is not better to leave people where they're happy but unsafe, rather than have them desperately unhappy and safe. And your mother was never one for sitting about looking at other old folk. She's been a live-wire all her life. I think that maybe we'll just leave her as she is just now. I'll give her a look in every now and again. And we'll have another talk in September, and see how she is. We'll maybe have to do something before the winter sets in. But she could easily be a whole lot better by then. We won't rush things.'

He agreed I could have a look round while I was in Glasgow, and see a few places which we might have to decide on if her condition grew worse.

Rhona had heard of a sort of guest house cum nursing home near Springburn Park and she thought it might be a good idea if I went in to see the lady one day. And I had heard of a lovely old house which had been turned into a proper home for the elderly out in Campsie Glen, and as my mother loved the country I thought we might have a look at it. I wanted her to come with me, for I didn't want to do anything behind her back, but she refused to come. 'It's not for now, Mother,' I urged her. 'It's just in case you want company for the winter. You can keep on your wee house as well.'

She was having none of it.

'I'm not going,' she said, staring at me as if I was an

enemy. 'Go yourself, but I'll never go into one o' thae places.'

Feeling like Judas, I left her and went out to Campsie Glen. It was a beautiful house, in extensive grounds, and the matron received me most warmly. But when she showed me into the lounge, where I merely put my head round the door, I knew my mother could never be happy there. A score or more of old ladies sat on hard chairs round the walls, staring into space, not speaking to one another, just waiting. Waiting for what? A meal? To die? For a loved one who didn't come? It was unbearable.

When I went round the lovely rooms, which were of a size and richness a hundred miles removed from the modest tenement rooms of Springburn, and with magnificent views over the wooded landscape, my spirits rose a little. In one room one old lady sat alone, staring out of the window. The matron introduced me, and then said, 'Why aren't you downstairs with the others, Mrs Brown? You shouldn't sit up here by yourself.'

Mrs Brown remained mutinously silent.

'Do you like it here?' I asked tentatively.

'No,' said Mrs Brown shortly.

'But there's a lovely view,' I ventured.

'Whit's lovely aboot it?' she said.

'Well, the grass, the trees.'

'H'm!' she snorted.

'Well,' I said desperately, 'what view would you rather have?'

She turned on me fiercely and barked one word, 'Folk!'

I knew with absolute certainty I could not ask my mother to transplant herself from the stir of Springburn to the safe tranquillity of this haven. It was folk she preferred too, and the liveliness of the mixed generations on a tenement stair.

I was more cunning with my visit to the guest house near Springburn Park, for my mother loved a walk round the park and the hot-houses. On the Sunday, I suggested a walk, and I pretended I knew a lady who lived opposite the gates who'd seen us both on many occasions out walking and who'd asked me to drop in the next time I was visiting my mother. I'd previously alerted the lady that we might pay her a short call, and hoped she'd co-operate, to allow *her* to have a look at my mother while *I* was assessing the possibilities of her house as a winter residence.

It was just like a private house, with no sign of a 'Home' about it, and the lady was busily preparing the lunch, with a fine aroma of roast beef coming from the kitchen when we went in. An old gentleman came down the stairs at that moment, and he could have been her father, so no suspicion was aroused in my mother's heart. With my mother's deafness she was used to my chatting quickly with people whom she didn't know, and so I was able to explain the situation swiftly and to ascertain that there might be a place for my mother in the winter. I arranged that the lady would in the meantime invite my mother for the occasional tea or lunch, so that if the time came when she had to move in for a longish spell, she'd feel she'd been invited by a friend. I'd settle the bills for teas or lunches, as provided, and any later accommodation.

My mother looked so pretty and so vivacious that I think this ex-nurse thought I was imagining the whole thing, but although she felt there was no urgency in extending a helping hand, I begged her to start the little casual invitations as soon as possible, just to establish a firm relationship before winter closed in.

And before I left for London, I also saw my mother's neighbour, and asked her to keep an eye on her, and if there was any expenditure involved, to let me know.

I told Rhona and Tommy all that had been done, and we agreed there was nothing more my mother would consider just then.

We also kept Willie and his wife Agnes in the picture, and asked them also to look in as often as possible, for they lived nearest to my mother, and Willie was my mother's favourite. Always had been. 'Willie's like me,' she would say, 'anything for peace.'

Tommy and I were 'right Weirs', she would tell us, in honest assessment of our ability to argue and discuss and stand up for ourselves.

'Aye, Mother,' I'd tease her, 'the meek may inherit the earth, but it takes the others to organize it for them!'

And then to make her laugh, I'd recall the visits of the old lady from the country with her daughter, a spinster of about forty. We were only toddlers at the time, and to us a spinster of about forty had one foot in the grave. Gazing round our Springburn tenement, she was loud in her praise of the virtues of this excellent daughter, from whom had been shielded all the rough facts of life. Always at the end she would lay her hand on her heart and exclaim, pointing the other hand at the pale silent woman, 'That wean never saw a bug!'

To us this statement was hilarious.

None of us had ever seen a bug either, and we could see no reason for mentioning such a thing.

But somehow to the old lady it implied a delicacy of upbringing which had to be shouted from the housetops.

It was of the same old woman's velvet toque that my mother said, with accurate if mystifying phrasing, 'Ah niver saw onybody that answered it as bad.' An interpreter might have enlightened the listener by explaining the meaning, 'I never saw anyone who suited it so badly.'

Somehow my mother's wording was pithy and to the point, and yet took the sting out of her criticism.

We had a jolly last evening, only disturbed by a party of drunks who caroused and sang a few yards down the road, obviously celebrating Glasgow Fair, which was just about to start. I stood it till I could stand it no longer, and then, verifying the time from my watch, I rose in a fury, marched to the window, threw it up, and checked their exact position. My mother meantime had wakened and joined me at the window. 'Whit is it?' she asked. Without answering her I filled my diaphragm as though about to deliver immortal lines from Shakespeare to the back row of the gallery, and shouted, 'Do you know what time it is? It's half past one in the morning. *Get* home to your beds at once!' If they'd seen the size of me, they'd not have moved a muscle, but my voice electrified them in the silence of the night. Silent but for them, that is, until I spoke.

'My Goad,' somebody said, 'it's half past one in the morning. So it is. Goodnight, Erchie. Goodnight, Wull. Goodnight, Davie.' And they'd gone.

My mother was hanging on the window sill laughing. 'My Goad, did ye ever hear onything like oor Molly's Sergeant-Major voice!' And then, more soberly, 'I'm gled ye didnae go doon, for they might have set on you.' As if I would be so daft. The unseen menace is always far more effective than visible wrath.

My mother decided she would come down to Central Station to see me off. For the first time for years, so did Willie's wife, Agnes. With my mother's deafness, conversation in public was always difficult, and in a quiet train with the other passengers sitting murmuring to one another or entirely silent, it was well-nigh impossible. One can't shout platitudes at the top of one's voice, and with us having been together for the best part of six weeks altogether, we'd exhausted all our real conversation.

Besides, with Agnes having made the effort to come to the station, I felt I had to talk to her and give her all the latest news.

My mother was always sensitive to being excluded from the conversation, although she knew in her heart that her hearing aid couldn't cope with the noises of railway stations plus the human voice, and she tended to shut it off. Agnes and I were really only uttering banalities, but all unheard exchanges seem far more exciting to the deaf than they are, and I could see my mother's face cloud with annoyance that I wasn't speaking more to her.

I was in an agony of mind, trying to be nice to both of them, and not succeeding one bit with my mother.

She was wearing the green coat we'd bought at the C&A sale in London, and the little velvet hat which suited her so well. Her skin was glowing and golden from her holiday with us, and I'd never seen her looking bonnier. Or looking more annoyed with me. I felt like a schoolgirl again, when I'd displeased her, and her look of disapproval could quench me.

She and Agnes left the train, and I called out, 'Cheerio, Mother,' and waved. But she was walking towards the exit and she didn't turn round. 'Mother,' I called, 'cheerio.' With her arm linked in Agnes's, she walked steadily on, without a wave or a good-bye.

My heart felt like lead when I went back to my seat, and I stared out of the window for many long miles before I could settle to read my book.

It had all gone wrong, somehow.

I felt as though I had the Stone of Destiny in my bosom, but I wouldn't cry. I turned with determination to my book again, but it couldn't hold my interest and I spent most of that journey gazing unseeingly out of the window.

In my case was the thistle crystal vase which she'd insisted I take back with me. There was an inch-wide sliver missing from one of the jagged thistle points, where she told me she'd 'dunted' it against the tap when she'd been washing it. 'Ah wis that mad at masel',' she'd told me, 'but ye haurdly notice it when there's flooers in it. Mind yer fingers though when ye're washin' it for it's like a lance.'

As I recalled her colourful way of expressing herself, my spirits lightened. In childhood, when I'd answer a summons with the words 'I'll juist be a wee minute,' how often had I heard her say scathingly, 'Aye, ah widnae like tae hing by my heels fur that wee minute.'

When being over-critical of something which had been made for me, I would be stopped short with her words, 'A blin' man wid be gled tae see it.'

When the wee dairy wife's daughter was married in the local church, with a reception in the City Bakeries up the road, it wasn't just a lovely wedding. Oh no, that was far too tame for my mother. She told me with glowing eyes, 'It was the wedding of the year.' Not for nothing was she a devourer of the newspapers, and if such descriptions were good enough for Mayfair, they were surely good enough for a Springburn wedding.

Springburn teemed with interest for her, and she had no desire to live anywhere else.

Och yes, I told myself, she has a marvellous spirit. This is just a temporary phase and the doctor will keep an eye on her. Indeed, he had visited her the day before I left, when I'd been doing a little shopping. She'd been down at the midden emptying the ashes, that time-honoured Glasgow custom, essential where folk all burned coal fires, and to her surprise she'd come in and found tall, handsome Dr Bissett, standing leaning against the mantelpiece, 'quite at home' she told me. 'Ah niver sent fur ye,' she assured him. 'Would you believe it,' she'd said, 'he was juist passin' and came in to see how ah wis gettin' oan. Wisen't that nice o' him?' No suspicion entered her mind that I had anything to do with it, and I felt very heartened that he had taken the trouble to have a look at her without delay.

By the time I reached London I'd assured myself that I'd erected a barrier between her and danger, and I looked forward to nothing more than a long spell of unbroken sleeps in my own bed, a holiday somewhere in the sunshine, and the autumn series of the Lyons' shows.

When we returned from our holiday, I had a booking for what sounded like a most interesting television play. They were doing a prestigious series called *These Names Made History*, and I was booked for the one concerning the life of Lister, the man who had devised the use of antiseptics in saving life and limb, in the bad old days where if a leg became infected as the result of a carelessly performed operation, they simply cut it off.

I was to be the nurse Lister brought with him from Edinburgh, to support all his judgments and help him carry out his treatments without interference from doubters.

There was a huge cast, for it was to be treated in documentary style, and Richard Attenborough was to do the narration. The splendid Robert Eddison was playing Lister, and with his lovely mellifluous voice, noble head, and gentle bearing, it seemed to me to be perfect casting.

We had a whole team of medical experts visit us from University College Hospital to show us exactly how to apply the bandages, and splints, as well as the correct manner of folding back bed clothes, and handling patients, to fit in with the period during which we'd have been doing such nursing.

It was utterly different from my part as Aggie, and I would just be able to fit it in before we started our series. Marvellous timing, and a great opportunity for me to play a serious part. We were to rehearse for three weeks.

Rehearsals were great fun, and I found Robert Eddison, in spite of his noble appearance, a source of great hilarity. He himself could keep his face straight while muttering terrible things under his breath, but he had me collapsed in giggles, just as I used to be when working with Gordon Jackson. He couldn't believe a disciplined actress like me could be 'corpsed' so easily (our word for breaking up in laughter), and he couldn't resist displaying his ability to have me collapse in uncontrollable chortles during the most serious parts of the play. I could have strangled him, and kept begging him not to tease me, or I'd surely burst out laughing during the actual performance.

The day before the dress rehearsal, when I reached Pinner, I felt how lucky I'd been to have had such lovely weather for the three weeks I'd had to travel right to the other side of London. And I hadn't even minded the travelling too much, for the whole play had been so interesting. I'd loved meeting Richard Attenborough at the later rehearsals when he came to fit in the lengthy narration, for I'd admired him for years as one of our most talented stage and film actors. I was delighted to find him so friendly and pleasant, and I was really looking forward to seeing the whole show come together in the studio, with us in our old-fashioned nurses' uniforms, using the old hospital beds, acting the drama of a break-through in medicine.

When we'd finished our meal, Sandy went out into the

garden to do some work there, and I began arranging the things I'd have to take with me next day to dress rehearsal. My knitting to pass the long hours as we set up for each scene, my vacuum flask in case I wanted coffee or tea in the dressing room and couldn't be bothered to go to the canteen, a box of sweeties, cigarettes, needle and scissors in case I finished my knitting.

And then the telephone rang.

It was Agnes, from Glasgow, and my heart skittered into my mouth, for she seldom rang us. 'I have bad news,' she said. And still I had no premonition that it was the worst possible news I was ever to hear.

'What is it?' I cried. 'What's wrong?'

'Your mother is dead.'

'She can't be,' I cried, 'she can't be dead.'

My immediate thought was that she couldn't have done such a tremendous thing without me being beside her.

She couldn't have gone on such a journey by herself, without my hand to hold her up. Agnes was wrong. It was a terrible mistake.

Agnes's voice was going on.

'When can you come up?'

'But what happened?' I kept insisting. 'What happened? How did she die? Was it an accident? She couldn't have just *died*, without warning, not my mother.'

By this time I was crying uncontrollably and I heard Agnes say to my brother, 'Bill, you'd better speak to her.'

I don't actually know why he hadn't done so in the first place, unless he felt a woman's voice would tell the awful tidings more gently.

When he came to the phone, I asked him through my sobs, 'What happened, Willie? Tell me what happened? How did she die?'

I felt this was the one thing I had to hold on to. If they gave me one concrete fact, I might believe it.

'She was gassed,' he said.

'Oh no!' and I let out such a scream of anguish that Sandy

heard me from the bottom of the garden and came running in.

He took the phone, told Willie we would ring back and held me close till I gradually quietened down.

Tears streaming down my face, I saw once more my mother turning away from me at Central Station without a backward glance. I couldn't bear it.

The word 'gassed' with its terrible undertones of suicide filled my mind. Could it have been because she was frightened of going into a home? Could it really have been an accident?

And then the words of her ditty filled the room,

> 'Ah wish ma maw wis here,
> Ah wish ma maw wis here,
> It's an awfu' thing tae dee alane,
> Ah wish ma maw wis here.'

And she had died alone. Which to me is a terrible fate. I know we must go into the unknown alone, but surely it is not too much to ask of God that we have a loved face as our last sight on earth?

And I had always wondered how I would be able to look on her dead face, at the moment of death, and this anguish was to be spared me. But only this anguish.

And then I remembered the television documentary on Lister. What was I to do? How could I rehearse and record with this horror draining me of strength and purpose? And yet I knew I had to. It was one thing asking anyone to step in at the last moment to learn the lines of a straightforward play. Many actresses can perform prodigious feats of memory and can be trusted to do such a thing. But how could anyone fit into a medical documentary with a cast of twenty-nine, and learn not only lines but all the procedure with bandages and splints and all the dozen and one little finesses we had been taught by the experts. I couldn't let everybody down like that.

Sandy rang Willie and told him we would see how I was in the morning, and that if it was felt I must and could do the play, we would be home on the Monday, for the funeral on Tuesday.

Willie said they would fit in with my timetables, for my mother lay in the city mortuary.

'God spare her the realization of where she is,' I prayed. The mortuary had always filled her with grief, at the mere thought of anyone having to be taken there either because the corpse was unknown or had nobody to care where it went.

And now she lay there, aloof and alone, because of the circumstances of her death.

We were getting ready for bed when the telephone began to ring again. It was the newspapers. They had got hold of the story and wanted my reactions. Aggie of *Life with the Lyons* was a national name, and this was headline news. I couldn't speak to them. Sandy dealt with them and then left the phone off the hook. I swallowed my Alka-Seltzers, but as on the night of the burglary which had started the trail which had led to this night, they were ineffective.

And as I lay and stared at the ceiling, letting the tears flow unheeded so that I wouldn't disturb Sandy, I kept remembering signs which I had not fully noticed. That day Sandy had returned from the office, when I was in Southampton, and had found the kitchen full of gas which she hadn't smelt. We had believed her when she said it was because she was sitting by the french windows in the dining room.

That day in Glasgow, before I had left for London, when I came back into the house after doing my stint of emptying the ashes, and found a gas tap turned on and the place heavy with gas. In my fright I had seized her and turned her head down towards it to make her smell it, and she'd said tetchily, 'You're very smart! It just blew out when you came in at the door. You know I'm feart o' gas, and I'm always careful.'

I had believed her.

Much much later when we talked it all over with Rose, Sandy's sister, and with another friend who often visited mother, we discovered that on many occasions they'd found a gas tap turned on, with deadly gas whispering into the room, and my mother, always hating to be found out being less than competent, and with an actress's skill in deception, had easily assured each and every one of them that the gas had just that moment blown out with the draught from the opening door.

She had kept it from all of us only too successfully, but she had gradually been losing her sense of smell. And, like most of us, she saw no danger in a tiny amount of gas. I think too that with the new gas cooker, with its newer taps which required to be pushed in, she may have come to believe that they ignited by the simple act of pushing the tap. After her behaviour during what was to be her last holiday with us, any sort of aberration was possible.

I would find out everything when I went home, but there was tomorrow to face.

In the morning, I rang the producer's secretary and told her, through tears, what had happened. I had, in the night, made up my mind what I was going to do. I told her that if she would inform everyone in the cast of the tragedy, and tell them that under no circumstances were they to refer to it, I would be able to get through the show.

Sympathy would shatter me.

A conspiracy of silence was what I sought.

I wouldn't have told anyone at all, but I was afraid the newspapers would carry a paragraph, even down here, and all I asked for was silence.

'But, Molly,' the girl said, listening to my sobs, which I was unable to control because I was speaking of it to her, 'you'll never be able to do it.'

'If you do your part, I will,' I said.

On the way to the studios, I went into a chemist and had him make me up a glass of sal volatile which I drank there and then, and it stopped the trembling and steadied me.

I felt an icy coldness round my cheeks and head, and the same numbed separation from all humanity that I had experienced after Grannie died.

When I went into the studio, everyone was very casual,

and beyond a brief 'Morning', went about their own business. I relaxed a little. It was going to be all right.

The only sign anyone gave that anything was at all unusual was when we went to queue for coffee at various times during that endless day. As I rose to join them, I would be pushed into my chair. 'I'll get it, Molly,' someone would say carelessly, 'you don't take sugar, do you?' With such small unobtrusive kindnesses they let me know I was being cared for, but no shattering word was uttered. Oh, I was so grateful to them.

Next day, the day of the recording, I found that I who normally spend a great deal of my time alone in my dressing room on such a day, couldn't bear my own company. The moment the need to be brave was gone and I was alone, scenes of my mother's death pictured in horrific, imagined, detail flashed before my eyes, and I began to tremble from head to foot.

I had to be with people to keep horror at bay.

So I sat with my knitting all day in the studio, through scene after scene, and I said to myself, 'After this, I can do anything. If I can do this, if God helps me to get through this day, He will never desert me at any future trial.'

And when the last shot was recorded, Richard Attenborough came over and kissed my cheek lightly, but said nothing. The others called, 'Good night, Molly,' and the producer said, 'Thank you.'

And I ran up the road to the tube, shaking with tears. It didn't matter now. I could let my sorrow overflow, and the next stage in the tragedy could be faced.

When we reached Glasgow, we went straight to Willie's house, as arranged. I had wanted to go to the Chapel of Rest in Springburn, where we knew my mother's body had been transferred, but the usual domestic details demand attention, and we felt Agnes might have gone to a lot of trouble to await our arrival with a meal.

Tassie was there, with some neighbours, and I had to exercise almost superhuman control to be able to speak rationally to them. 'How could we not see her?' Tassie wept. I stared at her. 'What do you mean, Tassie?' I asked. 'They won't let anybody see Jeannie,' she said. Jeannie was my mother's name. God help me, I thought, we are not to be allowed to look on her face again.

This had been decided as in the best interests of everyone, for gas poisoning changes the appearance, and it was felt it would be too distressing for us.

If only Tommy had been there, to have helped with such heartbreaking decisions, but he was in Greenland, climbing with Sir John Hunt, and he didn't even know what had happened. It was all part of the nightmare that he who had stayed with my mother long years after Willie and I had married, and who had cared and worried over her, and had found the flat for her, was now beyond the reach of telegram or telephone. Who would break the shocking news to him? And when would it reach him?

I longed to run from the room, and make my way somehow to Springburn, and force the men to open the coffin so that I could say my goodbye to my mother. I couldn't bear that my last memory was of her back, moving away from me. But I was too weak to resist all the arguments against it.

Mrs Dickson, Rhona's mother, our good angel who had been such a tower of strength after the burglary, came in the morning and helped to prepare the funeral baked meats. We were invited to have a lunch with a neighbour, but such socializing was beyond me. I had no appetite, and only wanted to be quiet. The little back room was filled with flowers, magnificent tributes from every part of Glasgow, and especially from Springburn.

Bebe and Ben had sent a telegram as soon as they heard of my mother's death.

> *Molly Darling, we are so upset to hear*
> *your sad news. Our love and prayers*
> *are with you. Please let us know if we*
> *can do anything. Love, Bebe and Ben.*

They sent a most beautiful wreath, like a perfect, round

cushion. It was all white, and it was made up of chrysanthe-mums, roses, carnations, gladioli and heather.

The card said, 'From Bebe, Ben, Barbara and Richard, for "Aggie's" wee Scottish mother' who, Ben once said, 'Talked nearly as much as her daughter did.'

The press saw my grief-stricken face and left me alone.

The fans took white carnations from Bebe and Ben's wreath.

My mother would have loved the flowers. As well as the florists' wreaths, we brought up a little nosegay of roses from our own garden in Pinner, the roses she had loved when she had visited us, and we laid them among the others.

Friends came, and neighbours came; workmates came too, right back from her young days in the sweetie factory, as well as colleagues from Cowlairs' Railway Workshops, and neighbours from all the tenement houses she'd flitted to during her long happy years in Springburn.

'Aye,' said one of them, 'she got a rare turn-oot.' A man pressed my hand. 'She was a lovely wee dancer. She was my favourite partner.'

'Aye,' said an old neighbour, whose wife, crippled with arthritis, was watching from her third-storey window opposite, sad that she couldn't be with us, 'They gave her a rare send-off.'

So we laid her to rest in the grave which held wee Jessie, and Grannie. And the sun shone from a cloudless blue sky and I felt my heart was broken.

9

The nightmares began when we returned to Pinner. There had been so much to do in Glasgow, that sheer exhaustion must have kept them at bay. We had the agonizing task of going through my mother's clothes and effects, and it seemed an intrusion. As I held the shoes I'd bought for her a few short weeks previously, I remembered a poem where a widow's grief only found release when she discovered her husband's old 'baffies', pushed out of shape with his bunions, thrust under a chair. They seemed such a living part of her dead husband, with the imprint of his feet, that she couldn't endure the pain of the memory.

So with my mother's clothes.

Her dance dresses, her jerseys, her cardigans, and above all her shoes. For, like me, she adored shoes and couldn't resist them.

Surveying shoes which hadn't even been on her feet, Sandy said to me, 'Don't die before me. I don't want to have to go through all this for you.'

Through my tears, I said I would try not to impose this task on him.

But there were more than effects to clear up. I had to find out, for my own peace of mind, what had happened. Her neighbour told me that she'd looked in on my mother every day, but that on the Wednesday she hadn't done so, because she thought my mother would be over visiting Willie. On the Thursday, she'd meant all day to push the door open to see how she was, but always something had got in the way. In the evening, having promised her wee daughter that she'd take her to the pictures because she'd passed an examination, she was half-way downstairs when she stopped and said to the wee girl, 'I must just take a look in at Mrs Weir before we go. I promised Molly, and I haven't seen her since Tuesday.'

She'd pushed the door open. It was 'off the sneck' as we say, with a newspaper to wedge it from blowing open, so that any visitor could just come in, for if my mother had not been wearing her hearing aid she wouldn't have heard the bell. When she crossed the threshold, she'd smelt the gas, thick and nauseating. My mother was lying on the floor where she'd fallen from the settee. The unlit gas jet was slightly turned on, and there was a small aluminium teapot half full of water standing on the cooker, with the tea-caddy beside it and a box of matches.

It was obvious she'd been about to make her morning cup of tea, had forgotten to light the gas, and had sat or lain down on the settee till the water boiled, and had fallen asleep.

Nobody had come to the door all day, and when they did it was too late.

The neighbour was in great distress. She needed comfort and I told her I had never expected more than a casual neighbourly eye, and that I fully understood people had their own lives to live, and she mustn't punish herself by any feelings of guilt. We can't make other people assume our responsibilities, and I had been more than grateful for the kindness and friendship this neighbour had shown to my mother. But she was haunted by the posters which had proclaimed to all Glasgow, 'Molly Weir's mother found gassed', and felt somehow she had contributed to the tragedy.

The lady who ran the guest house near Springburn Park wrote to me in great sorrow, apologizing for not having got round to sending even one invitation to my mother for tea. She too needed comforting. Time runs swiftly when one is busy, and how could she know that it had to be now, or fate would step in and make it never.

She couldn't forgive herself that she hadn't realized the

urgency of my appeal, but I told her she mustn't blame herself, nobody could have foreseen this tragedy.

Sandy begged me to leave it at that, but I couldn't. I had to know which day it had happened. Had anyone at all seen her on the Wednesday? How long had she lain there? It was a compulsion to know. When we went round to the factor's office to settle the rent, and tell them what arrangements we'd made, the girl behind the counter was sympathetic and kind, and I just kept talking and talking, looking for any sort of clue which might help me. And suddenly the girl had said, 'And I saw her on the Wednesday afternoon, when I was coming back from my dinner, and she looked so nice in her good green coat, but I thought she seemed very dreamy and far-away.'

So she had been alive on Wednesday afternoon. Thank God. Somehow it was terribly important to me to know that she hadn't lain neglected and undiscovered for two whole days. Sandy was looking at me, amazed that I had discovered this solid fact merely by holding the girl in conversation. But how else is memory stirred? A word, a hint, and a picture flashes before the inward eye which one may barely have noticed at the time

The Procurator Fiscal, aware of my deep distress, agreed to see me, and he revealed that the post mortem had shown she had had breakfast on that fatal morning. He also assured me it had been sheer accident, without a shadow of a doubt.

It was the stillness of that heavy August day which had contributed to the lethal effect of the gas. The door hadn't even been properly shut; there had actually been a little space at the top of the window, and the gas had been on the merest 'peep'. But it had been breathed in for too many hours, and no cleansing breeze had come to clear the air.

He knew what was in my mind

'Miss Weir,' he said, looking at me with steady, kindly eyes, 'it was an accident. We see many suicides, and people who wish to die this way make very sure of everything. They shut the door, they pack all the cracks with towels, and they turn on all the taps so it will be quick and certain. There was absolutely nothing like that in your mother's case. The neighbours sent for the police, and nothing was touched until they arrived, and both the police and the ambulance men confirmed that it was a classic case of accidental gassing.'

He knew I needed such facts to ease my mind.

I thanked him and knew I could now leave Glasgow truly believing that the verdict, of 'accidental death' was the whole truth.

Believing the facts was one thing. Coming to terms with the reality was much much harder. A neighbour had only to mention my mother when I was out shopping and I was racked with uncontrollable sobs. The wee keeper of our local park, with whom she was on very friendly terms, wept with me when he learned she was gone. Mrs Poupard would come rushing to the door when she would hear me crying through the thin walls which divided our houses. Such grief, so publicly expressed because I was unable to conceal it, is an embarrassment to people, and so I tried my utmost to impose a tight control on myself.

The result was the start of the nightmares.

My mother and I would be pursued by tigers, and I would be clawing them off her back, but as each one slunk away, another sprang to the attack and I grew weaker and weaker, unable to save her.

Another took the form of a sea trip in wild and stormy waters. We would be standing by the ship's rail, hanging on, and she would slip from my grasp into the deep waters.

She would be going along a train corridor, and a door would suddenly open, and as I raced to save her, she would fall to the track.

I would waken each morning, pouring with perspiration, tears coursing down my cheeks, and filled with such despair that I could scarcely summon up strength to face the day.

I grew so thin and white that people in the shops commented on my appearance.

I've never been very heavy, but my weight now dwindled to a mere six stone.

In the daytime, I could see and hear my mother in every corner of the house. I had only to look at the windows when I opened my eyes in the morning, to hear her voice, 'Aye, ah'll dae yer windaes fur ye before I go hame. They're such lovely glass, they're a pleasure tae dae.' This had been one of her self-imposed tasks, and now the 'lovely glass' would know her ministrations no more.

The needle with the thread still in it which she'd used to sew a button on a mere five weeks previously, lay on the dressing table and I couldn't bring myself to move it.

The hankie which she'd pushed below her pillow was still there. I felt if it was still crumpled from the pressure of her head, she was still with me.

Sandy, alarmed by the debilitating nightmares, insisted that I went to see the doctor. I realized he must really be worried, for he is not one to seek out medicos if he can get along without them.

The doctor was kind and very sympathetic. My weight and low blood pressure didn't bode well for a calm approach to life, and when I told him about the nightmares, he decided, with Celtic mysticism (he's Irish!) that I was being 'haunted'. 'You'll have to get out of that house,' were his final words, 'or you'll know no peace.'

We'd actually been looking off and on for another house during the previous year, for the buses had added our lane to their schedules, and where they came, the motor-bikes followed. What had once been a quiet and peaceful by-way had become a through road, and many a time and oft I'd been aroused from necessary sleep by selfish motor-bikes roaring past the window. Their ear-splitting din had ruined too many nights when I'd gone to bed early to be fresh for film work, and I had reluctantly decided we must move to a quieter part of Pinner.

However, every time we'd gone to look at other properties, Sandy had vowed he wouldn't consider moving for he hadn't seen a house as nice as the one we were in.

I didn't tell him what the doctor had said about moving to a new house, until he himself, looking at my white face a week or so later when the nightmares showed no sign of lessening, turned to me and said, 'I think we'd better start looking at houses again.' I then told him of the doctor's advice, and that settled it. The hunt was on.

The time had rolled round for us to make a start on the new Lyons' radio series, to be followed at once by the TV series, and it seemed strange and unbearable that these events should be beckoning, without my writing to my mother to tell her all about our plans.

For nearly fourteen years, since I'd first come to London, I had written to her every week, sometimes several times a week, no matter how busy I was, telling her everything I was doing. I knew how seldom deaf people are engaged in real conversation by friends and neighbours. It is too difficult and too embarrassing, and exchanges tended to get no further than 'How are you, Mrs Weir?' 'Oh, I'm fine, how are you?' 'Great. Cheerio then.'

So, knowing the general curiosity concerning everything to do with show business, I wrote to her the full details of my life, the rehearsals, the people I met, the dinners I attended, the clothes, the gossip, so that my mother could do most of the talking to acquaintances and chums who were delighted to find in her such an inexhaustible source of show-biz gossip and tit-bits. The handicap of her deafness was completely overcome in this enthralling and endless peep behind the scenes.

Only when she was gone did I realize the empty space which had been left by the removal from my life of this 'diary'. I had truly thought I was doing it for her, to enrich her life, but now I became aware that I had subconsciously been doing it for myself. And with a fresh stab of pain I realized something else. That the loss of a remaining parent is quite unlike any other bereavement. It is only then that one becomes truly adult to all the world.

For parents live through their children, and in your mother's eyes you are always a bairn and while she lives you know in your bones that however interested anyone else appears to be in your schemes and plans, it is only to her that every last tiny item is of riveting concern. She and she alone is never bored by the smallest details of your life, however trivial. A husband or a wife can be too busy to bother, children have their own absorbing world. The piercing emptiness of that special loss is that you gradually realize that never in your whole life is anyone ever going to be so utterly and wholeheartedly interested again.

I remember saying this to a fairly elderly chap at a dinner, who had complained all through the meal about his eighty-year-old mother because she still treated him like a child, and him in his fifties. 'She drives me up the wall,' he said, stabbing his meat angrily at the memory. ' "Now change your socks," she'll say when she suspects they're damp after a walk in the woods, "or you'll catch a cold." As soon as the wind blows she makes me put on a heavier shirt, as if I was an old man in danger of pneumonia, and although I loathe them she's always feeding me with eggs and cheese because she's convinced I'll dwindle and die without them in my diet.'

'Be very glad you have her,' I told him. 'While she's alive, you're still a boy. When she goes, you'll be an old man with nobody close enough or old enough to tell you off. You'll be in the elderly category then, and nobody will dare to offer you advice, even if it's for your own good.'

He swung right round in his chair and stared at me in astonishment. Then he said thoughtfully, 'My goodness, I never thought of it like that.'

I hope his old mother noticed his gentler and more conciliatory attitude next time he went to stay with her.

I was glad to escape from the frozen inertia grief imposes and plunge into the bracing activity of rehearsals, for the time had come round again for the next series of *Life with the Lyons*. Bebe and Ben and the family were very loving and understanding, and it was good to be with them, and find I could even begin to laugh at the jokes and argue over the script. I think Bebe would have thought I'd entirely lost interest in my work if at some point in the rehearsals I hadn't chipped in with, 'We wouldn't say that in Scotland.' She used to wink at the others when this happened, and all would lay down their scripts and stare at me, until I blushed to the tips of my ears. This particularly delighted Ben, who thought modern women had forgotten how to blush!

I was still very thin, but the nightmares were growing a little less frequent, probably because I felt I was solving that problem by continuing the search for a house. This was both time consuming and frustrating, as well as exciting and depressing by turns.

Sandy had got to the stage where he point blank refused to look at another house. He hated the business of walking round other people's properties and examining cupboards and kitchens. Far too many of them were in dire need of decoration and repair, in his opinion. He'd return from such visits and gaze appreciatively round our pristine home, and see only an immaculate quality which he felt we'd be mad to leave.

I kept urging him to 'get his eye in' by looking at enough houses to give himself a balanced judgment, but this reasoning cut no ice at all with him. He could never rid himself of an embarrassed feeling that he was 'prying' when he walked into strangers' houses, and I began to despair of ever getting him to look carefully enough at any property to come to a decision over buying it.

My TV series *Room for Improvement* had given me the detachment of an assessor, and I found I could tell almost at once the possibilities of anything we looked at. One day I went with a friend to look at a house of which we'd been given details from the house agent. It was situated in a lane which formed part of what was poetically described by the agent as 'rural Pinner', with its gas lamps, quiet tranquillity, and *very* expensive looking surroundings.

Isobel was an extremely well-to-do lady, with an eye for quality much more experienced than mine. When we stopped her little car at the gate, it was amazing how much she was able to take in with a single glance. I just saw the general shape of the house. She was murmuring approvingly of the quality of the heavy golden oak door, the lovely leaded lights, the conifer trees glimpsed at the back, and the fine wrought iron railings.

'Excellent design and quality, Molly,' she said at last, 'although it needs a lot of decoration, but that's an easy matter.'

Easy, did she say? Not if you had to pay a fortune for the property and hadn't another little nest egg in reserve!

The door was opened to us by a thin, white-haired old lady, who wore her coat and heavy boots indoors, and the house was absolutely perishing. It was a bitter November day, and I don't think she'd had a fire on for months. The very stones sent off a cold chill, and the house was packed as if she intended to move out next day. Linoleum was rolled up. Jars and packages were ranged in front of the fireplaces. Curtains were damp and stained. A huge crack ran up one wall, and there was a damp patch where a tank had overflowed at one time.

But Isobel and I were not deterred. The woodwork was of excellent quality, the shape of the rooms delightful, and the upstairs hall had been pared by the architect to a minimum, to release space where it would be far more effective, in the bedrooms.

A huge window in the back bedroom overlooked gardens devoid of any disfiguring fence. It was like one vast garden running right up to the corner of the lane, seven houses away. Even in November, it was a stunning view. The garden was long, with a greenhouse at the end, and a small sawn-off tree half-way up the lawn was topped by what turned out to be an ancient grinding stone. 'A perfect bird-table,' I thought to myself.

But the price was sobering, and I knew Sandy would see only the cracks and damp patches, and the yellow plaster unpapered walls in the hall. Also, for such a handsome property, the bathroom, although tiled for three-quarters of its height, was tiny compared with the one in our present house, and it was pretty gloomy, too. Sandy loved the large bright pink-walled sunny bathroom where we lived, and would consider this a poor exchange for such a costly house.

Isobel and I fell in love with the place, flaws and all, and the old lady was delighted with our feeling for the house. Over a cup of tea, we heard of how she had shared the house with her brother, and they'd been the first owners, for the house had been built at the exact moment they'd wanted to buy. That meant, as I well appreciated, that it had been taken care of by two elderly people and had suffered no real abuse. Like most older people, they hadn't spent cash on inside decoration, but had kept the fabric of the building well maintained.

They had gone to bed one night, he in the back bedroom, she in the front, as usual, and had called out their 'Good nights' to one another. And in the morning, when she rose to get a cup of tea for him, she found he had died in the night. Without a cry or a sign.

In my own emotional state, I wept into my tea with her, and she seized my hands in a feverish grip, because I think I was the first person to realize and share her loss.

As a house seller, she was her own worst enemy, for she had a miser's regard for the smallest item of expenditure, and would switch off lights, and sit in unwarmed rooms. We learned much later that she so terrified possible buyers with her witch-like hovering over them with wavering candles instead of electric light, that the gloomy corners looked much worse than they actually were, and they beat a hasty retreat without even putting in an offer.

I was very excited about the possibilities of this house, and the lane couldn't have been quieter. But when Sandy saw it, he was aghast. Especially when he was told the asking price.

'Look at that crack!' he kept saying to me, 'And I don't like that damp. And what about those big heavy brick fireplaces?' We were used to light, modern, tiled fireplaces, and the big Claygate beauties seemed to his eyes (and to mine, if I tell the truth) very gloomy and overpowering.

'We can always get new fireplaces,' I told him, 'I'll put everything I have into this house, Sandy, and we have our own house to sell and that can go towards a huge down-payment.'

'But every room would have to be decorated,' he protested, 'and we'd have to have a new sink. That old one in the kitchen is terrible.' My heart gave a lurch, as I remembered my poor mother's new sink and that gas-filled room.

He wouldn't budge, and I was almost in tears as I whispered to the old lady that he felt it was too expensive, and the house wanted too much spending on it, and we just couldn't afford it. She took my hands again and gazed into my eyes for comfort. 'But *you* like my house, don't you? You've said so from the beginning.'

'I *love* it,' I said, and as she was a spinster and I knew she would be on my side, I meanly added, 'but you know what men are like.'

We were two sisters together, and she squeezed my arm sympathetically.

Poor Sandy, and him one of the kindest and nicest chaps in the whole wide world.

That was in November.

It was a cold, unfriendly winter, with icy winds and black frosts, and we spent our weekends wandering round houses of all shapes and sizes and prices, and it seemed as though we would never find one which suited all our requirements.

December came and went.

January came and went.

We went farther afield, and when we'd go into agents' offices, and I'd glance through their list, my eye would fall on a description of the old lady's house, and I'd say, as though meeting an old friend, 'Oh there's our house.'

Sandy would say in irritation, for he was fast losing patience with this endless searching, 'What do you mean, *our* house?'

I noticed from the brochures they'd brought the price down slightly, so there had obviously been no offers.

And then one night in February, when we were heading for a cinema in a district within walking distance, we looked in at an agent's window and were attracted by an advertisement for a house in a street whose name we didn't know. It sounded interesting, and we decided that the next morning, a Sunday, we'd consult the big district map on display in our own village centre and check the address.

It was a dreich Sunday morning, mild and grey, and when we studied the map we discovered the address wasn't in Pinner at all. And the one point on which we were both agreed was that we didn't want to leave Pinner, which was bonnie, and which was handy both for London and for the country.

So, as we were out anyway, I suggested we take a stroll up the hill and have a look at some new houses which were being built at what seemed at that time vast expense. This building was taking place at the village end of the lane where the old lady lived.

When we reached the new houses, all Pinner seemed to have had the same idea as ourselves, and Sandy said, 'Oh, don't let's stop, or we'll never get anywhere, for everybody will want to have a chat.' One of the penalties of being in the public eye is that one can never be anonymous or pursue a quiet hobby anywhere without becoming the focus for attention. Flattering, but tiring at times.

So we continued through the lane. When we came to the old lady's house, we were on the opposite side, and we stopped and looked across at it. Sandy, whose eye by this time was well and truly in, said thoughtfully, 'It *is* a very handsome little house right enough.'

I leaped as if I'd been stung.

'Will I ring the bell and see if it's still for sale?' I asked, excitement running through me like electricity, for the first time since I had lost my mother.

'No,' he said. 'You're not ringing the bell on a Sunday, and anyway it's probably been sold long ago. It's three months since we looked at it.'

I stormed at him all the way home.

I could see the Holy Grail vanishing before my very eyes because of his obduracy.

'If people are selling a house they don't *care* if it's Sunday,' I yelled at him. 'They're only too pleased to see a possible buyer.'

When we reached home, he must have been chewing the whole matter over in his mind, because, reaching for the tattie peeler, he said, 'You ring the old lady while I do the vegetables, and see if we can come up after lunch.'

I sprang to the phone, and to my diary. By some quirk of fate, although it had been three months since we'd viewed that house, and I'd thrown out all the other brochures for houses we'd seen and rejected, I had kept that one single brochure, with the telephone number pencilled in, and I found it at once.

I dialled the number, my heart beating in slow sickening thuds. It had now become vital that we see the house while Sandy was disposed to consider it again. I felt I would collapse if she told me it had been sold.

We recognized one another's voices immediately.

'Is the house still for sale?' I asked. I couldn't frame the words 'has it been sold?' – I felt such words were too much in the past tense and I wanted present hope to colour my conversation.

'It is,' she said, sounding faintly angry, 'and I can't understand it. But I've had an offer,' she added.

'Can we come up and look at it?' I asked.

'Only if you're interested,' she replied.

I cupped my hand and whispered into the mouthpiece, conspiratorially sisterly again, 'I'm *terribly* interested, and we've just taken a walk past and my husband is so impressed by its handsome appearance he'd like to have another look. How about it?'

She was going out at three o'clock, she told me, but if we could swallow our lunch without delay, she would wait in for us.

When we reached the house, I drew her aside into the

kitchen. 'Leave me to go over the house alone with my husband,' I said, 'and I'll point out all its lovely qualities,' and I winked at her. She gripped my arm, 'You've always liked it, haven't you?' 'I've always loved it,' I said. I felt she adored the place herself, and it was important to her to know that someone who would possibly live in the place which had been so beloved by her brother and herself must not only see it as a roof over their heads, but must have affection for it too. I could understand such a feeling, for I share it myself.

Sandy and I wandered through the rooms, and this time after all the rubbish he'd seen, his eyes were open to their quality. He touched the ledges, he found the stairs had not a single creak as he walked on them, he swung the doors and their hinges were silent and smooth, and they closed of their own accord. The view from the upstairs bedroom captivated him, for the gardens were beginning to awaken. And when we walked to the end of the garden, and looked back at the house, he decided he liked the back view even more than the front.

There was just the question of price.

Sandy wanted to make an offer.

'Out of the question now,' I said. 'You're too late for such gambits. She's had only one offer. I'll bet you anything you like they've knocked her down to the even round figure of the nearest thousand. If we offer the asking price she must accept it. Otherwise with two possible buyers we'll be in a Dutch auction and the price could easily rocket away beyond what it was originally.'

I'd discussed houses so much in the previous three months, I knew all the jargon, and I was benefiting from everyone else's experience! I was trembling with nervous apprehension that Sandy wouldn't see my reasoning and we'd lose the house, for I just knew we couldn't go beyond the price she now asked.

Reluctantly, he agreed, and when we joined the old lady in the kitchen, I said, 'He loves it now just as much as I do. We'll buy it at the asking price.'

Would you believe it, the old rascal said, 'You wouldn't like to pay me the original price?'

Sandy said, 'I can't even afford *this* price.' And I said, 'Now you must be realistic. If you see a coat in Harrods and you go in to buy it, what would you say to the assistant if she said "You wouldn't like to give me an extra fiver?"' The old lady had been a school-mistress and she recognized logic when she heard it.

'All right,' she said, and put the kettle on.

Sandy sat and drank tea, while she and I had another weeping session over her brother and my mother, and if ever a bond was sealed over a wailing wall, this one was. I think poor Sandy could have seen both of us far enough.

But I felt it was fate. If we hadn't gone to the pictures and seen that advertisement, I kept telling myself. And if we hadn't gone to check the map. And if we hadn't then gone to see the new houses. And if the new houses hadn't been swarming with other people. And if we hadn't taken that stroll along the lane, and so on, and so on.

It was almost another nightmare to find myself going over and over this drama when my head touched the pillow of a night, and I trembled every time I thought of how nearly we had missed this dear little house.

For it had been a very near miss indeed.

The agent told me later that the single offer for the house had been made on the Saturday night. Because I was curious to know if I had guessed aright, he confirmed that my reasoning had been bang on target, and that the interested parties had indeed offered to the nearest thousand below the asking price. Thank goodness I'd managed to persuade Sandy not to start bargaining!

Because there had seemed no hurry, for the house had been on the market for five months without a nibble, the couple had given the old lady until the following Wednesday to consider whether or not she would accept their offer. They had felt there wasn't the slightest danger at this stage of anyone else showing any interest, and the house was as good as theirs.

But we had taken our fateful walk on the Sunday. We had made our firm commitment to meet the asking price on the Monday, and had set the wheels in motion immediately. When the unsuspecting buyers arrived on the Wednesday to confirm the deal, the house was gone!

Oh, I felt so sorry for them. For I know I'd have been devastated if I'd got so near to something I wanted, only to lose it. The agent said the lady buyer had rushed down to his office in tears, begged him to take a large sum of money for himself, and to offer the full asking price or more if only they could reverse the decision.

I greatly respected this gentlemanly agent when he told me how he'd informed the distraught buyer that the firm hadn't been in business over a hundred years, gaining the highest reputation for integrity and honesty, by following such practices as she suggested. There could be no question of the decision being altered. We had wanted the house sufficiently *not* to bargain, and that had settled the sale.

Truly, there is a time in the affairs of men when it is the best policy not to haggle.

Isobel was of enormous help in giving me the names of her workmen, and from that moment onwards it was all planning and measuring. I laughed the day I took the decorator along to measure the place before we ordered the wallpaper, for the house was so cold his hands trembled as he painfully wrote down the figures, and I could almost see the stubble of hair shoot out on his chin as his skin contracted with shivers.

The workmen were amazed at the way I could jolly this formidable old lady along, although there was one tense moment when she informed me that if the other lady had bought the house, *she* wouldn't have altered a thing, or even papered a wall, she would have come into the house just as it was! And only then did I learn that, having failed to move the estate agent, the disappointed buyer had visited the old lady and offered the only other bait she felt would work, a firm promise to leave walls and woodwork untouched so they could remain for an unspecified time just as in the old lady's day!

Oh gosh, that must have been tempting.

Seeing my dismay, the old lady patted my hand reassuringly. 'Don't worry,' she said, 'you always liked my house, and you gave me what I asked. I wouldn't have let her have it.'

Richard Lyon used to peer over my shoulder as I sketched in walls, and furniture, and ornaments, 'Are you still drawing that damned house?' he would ask. 'Yes, I am,' I'd reply. 'I've got to have it all worked out for the men.'

I went at it just as I had on the TV programme, and I had sketches, measurements, and colour schemes, all ready for the day when the old lady moved out and I could have a council of war with decorators, carpenters and electricians. But all that was three months ahead.

Meantime we were busy on our Lyons' TV programme, and we were advertising our own house for sale, and arranging for bridging loan, mortgage, and all the usual plethora of paper-work attendant on property deals.

Sandy was left to do most of the selling, and showing people round the house in the evenings, while I was out rehearsing, and I was endlessly engaged in keeping the house tidied and immaculate for prying eyes. I never had such a tidy airing cupboard in my whole life, or such a neatly organized kitchen. I don't normally put away used cups and saucers after every meal, feeling life is too short for such perfection, but now everything had to be hidden behind cupboard doors to show the place at its best.

We were frantically working out ways and means of meeting this enormous house purchase, and its later upkeep, and all our calculations were based on my thriving contract with the Lyons. We had now been running for ten years and there seemed no reason why we shouldn't run for another ten, for the show was as popular as ever.

The last of the present TV series was just coming up, and it had all been very successful. Critics and public alike approved of us, and I had been very glad of the work to keep me fully stretched during this trying period of my life. When this show was 'in the can' I'd be able to devote myself to the move to the new house. It was all working out beautifully.

On the day of the last recording of the series, we broke for tea as usual, and when we came back to the studio somebody was holding an evening newspaper. In banner headlines, I read, '*LIFE WITH THE LYONS* COMES TO AN END. BEN LYON JOINS ASSOCIATED REDIFFUSION IN TOP EXECUTIVE JOB AT TEN THOUSAND A YEAR'.

I stared at the words, not taking them in properly.

'What does it mean, Ben?' I asked him, for he was standing in front of me.

'What it says, honey,' he replied. 'I've taken a job as an executive, and I can't work for myself as an actor.'

'But, Ben,' I said, 'when is the series coming to an end? I've just bought a house, thinking we were going on as usual.'

He knew about our house purchase, of course, for I'd never stopped talking about it since we managed to get it.

'I know,' he said, 'I couldn't let the news out. I was bound not to. *Life with the Lyons* finishes tonight!'

And that's how I discovered that the last of the series was not quite that. It was the last Lyons' show we would ever make.

I had an overdraft of five thousand pounds, and we were moving to a new house. And I had no job.

But there was no time to brood. I had far too much to do .

10

I threw myself with enthusiasm into the business of changing houses. If I had no work of a professional nature, at least I would have all the time in the world to devote to this expensive and exciting change over. For the first time for over ten years, I could allow myself to give complete concentration to one task, knowing I would not be interrupted by rehearsals or performances.

The workmen had all noted the essential dates in their diaries, and I had decided, with Sandy's approval, we would remain in our old house for two extra weeks, so they could work in an empty house and not have to pack up their tools every night. We estimated two weeks under such ideal conditions would give them all the time they required.

So when the old lady moved out, not without the final drama of a feverish illness which saw her sending for me, and clinging to me with pathetic dependence, poor soul, we had a council of war on the Sunday morning in the empty house.

First, the decorators. I handed them their colour schemes, told them when the wallpapers would be arriving, and introduced them to their fellow-workers. Then the electricians were given their instructions; and time-tables were agreed with the carpenter. The carpenter was a most droll chap. Tall and lugubrious looking, thin as a matchstick, he was a craftsman to his finger-tips. He cocked a quizzical eye on me when I handed him his notes and illustrations. 'Gorblimey,' he said to his apprentice, 'she knows what she wants all right. I only hope *we* can deliver the goods!'

I was to be the progress chaser and see that they all fitted in with one another, and any difficulties would be referred to me. All very businesslike, and I was thoroughly enjoying doing my interior decorating, à la the TV programme, only *this* time the BBC wouldn't be footing the bill, we would.

I had also arranged for the new telephone to be installed right away, so they would be on the other end of the line if I wanted to speak to them, or they wanted to do any ordering or check on any instructions. The carpenter christened me the Mighty Atom, just as my old boss had in the far-off days in my office job in Glasgow, and when I'd say to him, apropos any outstanding decision, 'I'll give you a ring,' he would lift his lugubrious face and say, with a wink, 'Make it a Bravingtons.'

But they were a marvellous team, and although Sandy had warned me not to be visiting the new house too often and annoying them, I was touched beyond words when I rang them one day to ascertain if some material I'd ordered had arrived, and they said, sounding very crestfallen, 'Aren't you coming up to see how we're getting on?'

Fifteen minutes later I was with them, and I knew from the barely concealed smiles and nods to one another as I rushed from room to room admiring their progress, that my enthusiasm pleased them. Everybody needs an audience! And from that moment I went up every other day, and the changes took place almost before my eyes, and thrilled me to my toes. I had never planned a whole house like this, changing every room, decorating every wall, and freshening and re-colouring the paintwork, and I was really having a ball. I had reckoned that there was so much to be done with the shabby interior that it would have taken Sandy and me an entire year to accomplish it, for we'd only have had week-ends and the few hours in the evening after he returned from the office. It was far better not to grind ourselves into the ground with this hard work, and lose a whole summer working indoors. Much better to pay workmen, however expensively, and let us concentrate on the garden and give ourselves the pleasure of working out of doors in the fresh air.

'After this,' I told Sandy, 'we'll keep it all clean ourselves.'

We had chosen the removal people with great care. They were a local firm who advertised on the cinema screens, and I felt they looked nice and reliable. Also their price was right. Sandy bought in cans of beer to refresh them, although I felt they would prefer tea, and I may say that I was right and those cans of beer lay untouched for the better part of two years, for we're neither of us very interested in such beverages.

There was hilarious proof of our lack of interest in alcohol when they lifted a chianti bottle we'd made into a lamp, and laid it carefully on its side in the packing case. Out poured a good half-pint of the liquor which had been left in the bottom of the bottle, and saturated everything else in the case!

As I suspected, it was tea which they preferred. And they drank it by the pint, for it was a boiling hot day, and perspiration poured off them. When we reached the new house, they laid the dining room carpet first, and placed everything on it, and half-way through the unpacking I stopped and made more tea for them. Lo and behold, the youngest of the men dropped his whole cup of tea over the fitted carpet!

Every time afterwards when we'd go to the local cinema and their advertisement came up on the screen, depicting them carrying furniture from van to room, and placing everything in its appointed spot, as soon as the young chap appeared, I'd point a finger at the screen and hiss, *sotto voce*, for Sandy's benefit and to make him laugh, 'That's the perisher who dropped a hale cup o' tea ower my guid carpet.'

It had all worked perfectly, and had really been a miracle of organization. Even when the electrician had discovered, literally at the eleventh hour, that the hot water pipes had been installed following a very old system which required the services of a plumber before he could connect up the immerser, I was able to enlist the services of the local plumbers on the very morning of the flitting. I realized that while we packed at the old house in the morning, they could be working on the pipes in the new house, and I impressed upon them that they must be out by one o'clock.

They were. Oh, happy days, when such efficiency was possible!

My lugubrious carpenter informed me that I was the first woman he'd ever met who'd been able to plan a schedule which worked. 'And do you know why it worked?' he asked me. 'No, tell me,' I said, flattered beyond words at his praise. 'Because,' he said, gazing at me admiringly, 'you *never changed your mind*.'

How I wished Richard Lyon could have heard him. For, of course, it was precisely because I had planned and worked out every detail for months before work actually started, that I wasted nobody's time with last-minute changes.

And in our eyes it looked beautiful. It was completely transformed. White paint gleamed where dark brown had oppressed the eye. Beautiful wallpapers enriched the rooms, lovely curtains hung at the windows. The kitchen had been completely renewed, with a new stainless steel sink, built-in wall cupboards, and pale grey tiled floor with random tiles in yellow, black and red.

We had at last found a splendid use for the card-table which we'd bought all those years ago with some coupon gift offer plus a modest sum, for the carpenter had covered it with formica to match our work-tops and it became our kitchen table. Of excellent quality, firm as a rock, we use it to this day.

And, because of my prudent Scottish ways, he had peeled the green baize top off most carefully, and had used the baize to line the knife drawer in the fitted cupboard by the sink. Oh, most excellent man!

Even our little fold-away stool was covered with left-over formica, so nothing was wasted.

It was just as well, for when I went up to the bank to complete the last transaction, I was surprised to see that the final figure on the sheet had been written in red. I noted it without taking in its significance, until from nowhere the words floated into my consciousness, 'In the red.' Red!

That's what it meant, literally, to be in the red – that the figures were written in red ink!

I gasped. 'What does that mean?' I asked, pointing at the figures, which seemed to be dancing in flaming lights. 'Oh,' said the teller comfortably, 'you're just a little overdrawn, but we're not worried, you've been a very valued client for many years.'

'But why didn't you tell me?' I gasped, 'I'm out of work. You shouldn't have *let* me. I've been writing cheques by the dozen.'

I had been so used to being solvent for so many years, that it never occurred to me my funds had evaporated, like snow off a dyke.

It was back to square one.

Sandy had always said, measuring the house against his salary, 'I can't really afford to live in a house like this.'

Now it looked as if neither of us could!

Ah well, as Willie McFlannel was wont to say, 'We never died a winter yet!'

We owed not any man so far. Just the bank.

And they would wait.

And I would surely get work.

But I didn't.

I was far too identified with the part of Aggie in *Life with the Lyons*, and nobody was at all interested in my services. Although I didn't know it at the time, it was to be all of thirteen months before I earned a single penny.

But just then, we were so busy settling into our new background, it was bliss to have the time and freedom to give our home our full attention. It was a glorious summer, and with the contrariness of human nature, although this move had been made to take me away from the other house with its painful memories of my mother, the moment we had the house straight, I kept thinking how much she would have loved it, and was filled with a passionate regret that she would never see it.

Suddenly all the emotional upheaval of the past few months caught up with us and we found we were snapping at one another. We only had Sandy's pay, but I said, 'Sandy, we're not enjoying this lovely house because we're too tired. Let's go away for a week, and we'll come back and see it all with new eyes.'

A friend had just returned from Wales and she had taken note of an inexpensive little guest house, which she'd passed on to me. I rang the lady. 'Have you a spare double room for next week?' I said. She had a cancellation for the following week. 'Right,' I said, 'we'll see you on Saturday some time.'

'You'll put it in writ-ing,' her Welsh voice sang down the line. 'I will,' I assured her, and turned from the phone with shining eyes. 'We're off first light Saturday morning, my lad,' I said. 'Eight guineas a week all in.'

It was a marvellous holiday. We drove up in our wee Morris, so no train fares had to be met. And it was the first holiday since our honeymoon that Sandy was proud to say was paid for entirely out of his pocket. For I was stony broke!

Sixteen guineas for the two of us for the week, plus a few pounds for petrol, and that was all we spent.

The sun shone, the rivers sparkled, and the air was like wine. We actually climbed Snowdon, quite accidentally, but that's too long a story to tell you here. The food was excellent. At the end of a week, we felt like giants, refreshed. We had sloughed off tiredness like an old skin, and we felt better than we had for months.

When we got back, the house looked absolutely splendid in our eyes. We were so new-fangled, we put on all the lights, and ran round it, gazing into each window to admire it from the outside. Sandy said, 'Never in my wildest imagination could I have visualized the changes you could make in what seemed a dark, dull house.' I was very happy.

He, incidentally, had changed his tune about the Claygate fireplaces the moment he went to have a look at the prices of replacements. He'd been seeking light, modern, tiled ones, and discovered to his amazement that in every firm he'd visited, the most expensive fireplaces in stock were Claygates. More than twice the price of anything else.

'I told you,' I said smugly, for I'd been doing my own investigating. 'Everything in this house is of top quality, and I can soon brighten them with my bits and bobs of brass and silver.' Which I did, and they looked handsome and rich, and not dull at all.

We threw ourselves into the business of reclaiming the garden. The old lady's brother had been a keen gardener, and there was a fine lawn, but, with all cultivated land, the moment the tending hand is removed, the jungle takes over. There were weeds down each border taller than myself, and I dislocated my finger yanking them out. It was like an archaeological dig. We discovered paths we didn't know existed, and a circle of stones with a broken ornament which we rebuilt to hold a vase. We dug and we tilled and we planted, and I for one was delighted with the size of our new territory. When the phone rang though, and I was at the top of the garden, I felt like Roger Bannister doing the four-minute mile, I had to put on such a turn of speed to get to it before it stopped. In the end I had to have an outside bell, and warn all our friends to give me time to get to the kitchen from the greenhouse. I had also to move the phone to the kitchen, the nearest point at the end of my sprint, to save the extra yards across the hall to the dining room.

But by far the most wonderful item in this new house was the downstairs toilet. We had one upstairs *and* one downstairs. To one who in childhood in Springburn had to share a stair toilet with fifteen people, opulence could go no further!

In the midst of all this domestic rejoicing, there nagged at the back of my mind the thought that I ought to be doing something about my career. It surely couldn't have ground to a complete halt with the end of *Life with the Lyons*. And yet the fact was inescapable that not a single telephone enquiry had come my way since the show had so dramatically and suddenly ended.

While I was pondering my future, I noticed in the newspaper one day a paragraph which told me that the Royal Academy of Dramatic Art (RADA) was having refresher courses for professional actors, and letters of application should be sent to so-and-so before such-and-such a date.

I stared at the advertisement with sparkling eyes. Here was a wonderful chance of doing something with fellow enthusiasts who spoke my language. It's absolutely no good being a Bernhardt at the kitchen sink. An actress needs an audience as a bank needs money. Without her public, she shrivels and becomes less than herself.

Even if it were spending money instead of earning, this course was almost bound to be stimulating.

I reached for pen and paper and the letter was in the pillar box at the end of the lane within half an hour. After a few days the reply arrived. Yes, they would be delighted to include me in the course. Would I just fill in the enclosed form and state whether it would be voice alone, or voice and movement I wanted. Fees were stated, and I noted there was a reduction if one took both classes, but to my amazement I discovered the classes were to be held every day, including Saturdays. This I hadn't bargained for. It wasn't going to be a pastime, it was a full-scale marathon I'd let myself in for.

I had clearly grown self-indulgent with too much time to devote to domestic chores, for I couldn't imagine how I was going to fit in shopping, cooking, washing, ironing, and so on, and so on, with daily classes. I, who used to do all these things on top of rehearsals and recordings! It was very obvious I needed a jolt.

'It will be very good for you,' I told myself, 'having to get up at a set time every morning.'

But 'myself' wasn't too pleased to be told this, for classes started at 10 a.m. in London, and the set time I'd have to arise unwillingly from my bed would have to be around 7.30 a.m. But there would be no turning back. The alarm *and* Sandy would arouse me at the appointed hour, and off I would go, with all the other commuters.

Came the first morning, and the crack of an icy dawn saw me scurrying down the lane, carrying my little bag with slippers for the movement class, ready for anything.

I sped along Gower Street about an hour later, in company with students and nurses, all racing for various universities and museums. It was the oddest feeling, like going back to school again, but quite enjoyable now I was fully awake.

A little notice inside RADA's famous portals gave a list of names of those taking the professional classes, and my name was in the group against Room 1. I felt a bit shy as I went in, but my tremors were quite unnecessary for there wasn't a soul to be seen. Huge no-smoking notices froze my hand on its way to my cigarette case.

After about ten minutes, a very pretty girl arrived, followed by two more, and they all knew one another. Completely ignoring the notices, they all lit cigarettes. 'It says no smoking,' I ventured. They stared at me in astonishment, then laughed merrily. 'Aren't you a law-abiding little thing,' the pretty one said. Next moment the door opened, and the teacher came in. And the cigarettes were stubbed out!

We waited for about five minutes while a few others drifted in. Then roll call was taken. One was the juvenile leading lady from the Frankie Howerd show *A Funny Thing Happened on the Way to the Forum*. She turned out to be a Scot, with lovely red hair, called Jean. My mother's name, with my mother's colouring.

There was a dancer from the Max Bygraves' show, anxious to learn how to speak lines and who, to my amusement, wanted to cultivate the sibilant 's' that most Scots find so distressing at the microphone. I tried to talk her our of her crazy ambition to hiss her esses, but she wouldn't be deterred.

Then there was Marilyn, an actress from *The Right Hon. Gentleman*, whose jaw had a disconcerting habit of practically dislocating itself when she breathed in a certain way. I recognized this as one more manifestation of the traumas afflicting one who is in a long run!

And there was Jane, straight from school, who later kept

us enthralled with tales of her mother's temper in the mornings! I thought I was thin until I saw this model girl in the changing room. She had the figure of a ten-year-old tall skinny boy. She was a darling, utterly unselfconscious, and the contrast between the glamorous clothes she modelled and the ones she wore to classes had to be seen to be believed. She turned up at RADA in skin-tight shabby jeans, fastened rakishly at the waist with a huge safety-pin because the buttons had all come off. These were topped with a boy's loose denim shirt, and her long legs were encased in rubber Wellington boots. No coat, no hat, even in bitter weather. Dead pale face, and lots of mascara encircling huge blue eyes, and a colourless mouth without a trace of lipstick. A kookie beauty, and I wondered how she would develop as an actress.

After her first show, the critics said of her, *She is so endearingly bad, you can't help liking her.*

Who could have foretold she'd go on to marry a top musician, divorce him, make one of the sexiest records ever to come out of France, all heavy breathing, and then live without benefit of clergy with a top French personality and have two children by him.

When I see her discussing free love and much else on TV I can hardly believe I once shared classes with her when she was a young, long-legged, coltish child.

The fifth member of our group was an actress from the TV series *The Avengers*, keen on developing resonance as a change from all the intimate delivery required for the small screen. Number six was a Shakespearean actress who had temporarily retired to have two babies and was now polishing her technique prior to attempting a come-back in the theatre.

Number seven was a West End actress who had been out of work too long, and, of course, there was me.

Four of them had been to RADA as students, and I was so thankful the model and the TV actress hadn't, because that gave us a fellow-feeling and made me feel less of an outsider. Although I must say we weren't made to feel that way at all. There was a faintly surprised admiration for what I, at least, had achieved *without* RADA and a great friendliness all round.

We all confessed we were terribly nervous, and were just starting our breathing exercises to find out what ghastly habits we had cultivated during our years as working actresses, when the door opened and in crept Fenella Fielding. I had never met her, but because I liked her zany comedy and had seen her so often in shows I felt I knew her, so I whispered 'Hullo' as she sat down, obviously embarrassed at being late and trying to pretend she'd been there all the time.

She took off the dark glasses she was wearing, put on an enormous pair of ordinary spectacles and whispered in return, 'Hullo, darling. Who is it?' To my relief, when I murmured my name she appeared to recognize it and gave me a radiant smile.

Meanwhile the rest of the class were clutching diaphragms, and prodding gingerly to see if the breath was reaching the lowest depths, and I tried to cope with sitting with the spine rigid but the shoulders relaxed. As we breathed, we were exhorted to purse our mouths like pigs, then rabbits, and in the middle of this pantomime Fenella's eye caught mine and our breathing went all to pot as we snorted with laughter.

How I ever earned my livelihood as an actress, I'll never know, for my breathing simply refused to leave my upper chest and descend to its proper place in the lower lungs. But I was a wee champion at sitting with my rib cage erect, although the rigid matching shoulders were a bit of a handicap, while the model beside me slumped and sagged like a concertina.

At the end of this session, all of us, spoiled actresses that we were, looked expectantly for coffee. But we were in school now, not rehearsal rooms or studios. Not a drop was forthcoming, and we trailed off to movement, thirsty and mutinous.

But movement, which was all directed towards muscle

toning, was so enjoyable we soon forgot our sulks over the absence of coffee. For a solid hour and a half we learned to move our muscles with great subtlety, not a jerk to be seen, and I must boast that to my delight I was fairly well limbered, and didn't feel too sore. It was only when we came to exercising the huge stomach muscle independently that agony set in, and later that night I moaned softly in my sleep when I tried to turn in bed, feeling as though I'd been kicked in the stomach by a horse!

Next day, we were schoolgirls to the manner born. Fenella was late, and, of course, was all at sea with an exercise we'd been shown before she crept in. 'We had it before you arrived,' I whispered smugly. 'Oh, you are *sickening*,' she hissed back. Gales of laughter at this childish behaviour, which we both acted to the full, I may say.

Then our teacher, capitalizing on this exchange, gave us a glorious insulting exercise, making us top each other in volume. 'Villain,' breathed Fenella. 'Murderer,' I called back. 'Assassin,' she roared. 'Parricide,' I yelled.

'What does parricide mean,' whispered the model next to me. 'The murder of one's father,' I answered hurriedly. She shuddered. 'Could I say to somebody, you are a parricide?' she asked. 'No,' I whispered. Then, as I caught the teacher's eye, 'I'll explain later.' And, of course, when I looked up the dictionary I found I was wrong. You could say it. I tended to get parricide and patricide mixed up, but she thought it marvellous I knew such a word at all.

I don't know why we should have bothered to whisper for nobody could have been less alarming than our charming instructor, but there was something about sitting in class, sitting stiffly in a circle in chairs, which aroused the craven in all of us. Even Fenella blenched when caught talking during an exercise.

Next day, the movement class became a bit more adventurous, and when I whirled round obediently as commanded, I found myself staring at a bare male torso, whose lower half was encased in pale blue tights. I *must* have been taking the class seriously, for this apparition had been beside me right from the beginning of the lesson and I hadn't even noticed! Perhaps it's part of the egotism or the concentration of the actor that he becomes less curious about those around him than the average student would be. It is a fact that during the whole four weeks' course, talkative as I am there were a handful of students with whom I didn't exchange a single word. They were little islands, intent on improving themselves, and other people simply didn't exist for them.

The loveliest part of movement was lying down on the floor at the end of each session, and giving oneself up to complete relaxation. I'd never been able to do this properly, but the exercises must have helped, for even on the hard cold floor, with a draught whistling under the door, I could have drifted off to sleep. I enjoyed this so much that I dreaded the teacher's voice breaking the spell with the words she used each day, 'Lie and think about getting up.' Then, 'Now *don't* think about it, and *get* up.' It was as bad as the alarm clock in the morning, and just as unwelcome.

The room where we changed had the words *Girls Cloakroom – Upper 2* painted on the door. It reminded me of the *Girls' Own Annual*, but I'm sure no schoolgirls behaved quite like us. One day when we dashed in to put on our street clothes, Fenella's dress was lying in a crumpled heap on the floor. She looked at it lying there, all abandoned and dusty, then said with great drama. 'Some *swine* has knocked my dress down and left it lying. I don't expect her to own up, but I hope she is *consumed* with guilt.'

Then having got it out of her system, she calmly dressed in the crumpled garment, and added what looked like half a pound of mascara to her three pairs of eyelashes, and applied more eye-shadow to eyes already mournfully ringed with black and brown make-up. I couldn't decide what I liked best, Fenella's dotty behaviour or the discipline of daily classes. I found both quite entrancing.

I must say we weren't a bit self-indulgent. We lay on the floor with feet propped on chairs during voice classes, until it became almost an agony of discomfort and we longed to get up. We stuck it to the last breath, almost literally, so that our breathing would be perfect.

We leaped, and skipped, and stretched in movement until every separate muscle ached and we tottered in next day feeling like very old ladies and gentlemen. Hair which had been shining and bouffant when we entered, was limp and flat with perspiration after an hour or more of muscle toning. 'I must say it's a little *depressing*,' Fenella would wail, 'having to go out and face one's public looking like this. One *really* ought to wear a wig.' This was long before wigs were part and parcel of any self-respecting actress's wardrobe, and Fenella showed great foresight in anticipating this need.

Although most of us had gone on this course mainly for the sake of the voice classes and had taken movement more or less as a lark, we found to our surprise that we wouldn't have missed the movement classes for anything. We loved the rhythm and the flowing movements, and we certainly learned to relax, which for me at any rate was extremely valuable.

As far as voice classes were concerned, I found that in the short time available we were more or less covering old ground, but re-discovering things we had perhaps forgotten and disciplining our breathing again. It's very easy to develop bad habits in the rush and bustle of a working life.

I think we all of us enjoyed the stimulus of reciting great passages of Milton instead of the humdrum dialogue common to a lot of kitchen-sink plays. Fenella and I would stand opposite one another, gazing with great hauteur into one another's eyes as we declaimed,

> 'Queen of this Universe, do not believe
> these rigid threats of death. Ye shall
> not die. How shall ye? By the fruit?
> But I also have eaten of the fruit and
> yet live.'

Even when we were dressing, the words resounded in our ears, and we would shout out this passage with great fervour, clutching our diaphragms and breathing in all the right places, until we'd collapse in helpless laughter.

It was a mad, carelessly happy interlude

And then suddenly it was all over.

And I discovered something about myself I'd always faintly suspected but never really knew for certain. My true vocation in life was to be a pupil. These four weeks had been among the happiest I had known. Not a means to an end at all, as I had imagined, but almost an end in themselves.

Goodness knows when I would get a job, so that I could put all that breathing and all those relaxed muscles to the test.

But there was nothing to stop me intoning, at our new kitchen sink, 'Queen of this Universe, do not believe these rigid threats of death.'

And then a strange door opened for me

A. E. Matthews, my old colleague and well-beloved eccentric actor, died. As I have told elsewhere,* he and I shared digs on tour and became good friends, and there were many personal tales of him which only I knew. I wondered if any newspaper would be interested in a little anecdotal write-up of him from someone who knew him fairly intimately as a colleague, and suddenly I remembered a party I'd gone to some months previously where I'd met the London editor of a Scottish weekly. He'd given me his card and told me then, that if I ever had anything which I thought would be of interest to their Scottish readers, I could send it to him

It felt good to be writing again, and I sent off the piece, and he in turn sent it to the Dundee office.

As Matty had died on a Friday, the weekend press had covered all the essential details, and my piece would have to have waited for another whole week before it could be included. And as somebody else has almost said, a week is a long time in journalism, particularly topical journalism.

However, the Dundee editor hadn't realized I had ever

* *A Toe on the Ladder*

done anything apart from *Life with the Lyons*, and he asked me to send him a synopsis of my career to see if he could fit something else in.

They were running a six-weekly series on various top theatrical personalities, and had struck a low patch as far as interest was concerned. The actor they had intended featuring to follow the current one, was a fine performer, but a dull dog in his other aspects. I fell into their lap at just the right moment, and they decided to serialize my life story instead.

Their London reporter came out to the house, and I more or less dictated the whole piece which, as I am a bit of a writer myself, was nae bother.

When the series was published, not only was it a pretty fair success, but the Dundee editor decided he liked my style of writing, which he considered fitted their public very well, and he wondered if I would consider becoming a regular contributor, doing a weekly piece of around 1000 words.

It could be on any theme I chose.

What would I suggest?

I sat and pondered. If I chose a specific theme I would be hard put to it to find a new angle every week. I knew from *Shopping Flash* that a regular writing commitment is both taxing and demanding, and I wanted to find something which I could fit into an acting life when my career picked up, as it surely must one day.

And then I thought of all the people who never receive a letter either from friends or relatives.

And of all the mothers whose children leave home and who lose touch with them.

And of the many people living in remote places, who never visited a theatre, and to whom a train journey was an adventure.

And of my mother, to whom I used to write of all my wider adventures every week until the day she died. Indeed, on my last letter to her, suggesting that she visit the lady round the corner near Springburn Park, she had written, in her own handwriting in the margin of my typed sheet, 'Go and visit Mrs So-and-so up Balgray Hill.' She was dead when I read those words.

And I knew what form my contribution would take.

It would be a letter from Molly, and I would write it exactly as I did to my own mother. When I was working, it would be about actors and rehearsals, and when I was not it would be about the house, the garden, the neighbours, and the odd recipe for a favourite dish.

The terrible blankness which had followed my mother's death would be filled, and in a sense it would be a sort of immortality for her. Because it would be to her I would really be speaking.

The time, the loved one and the opportunity had coincided.

I had come full circle, from that first article written and published by the *Glasgow Evening Times* at the age of fifteen.

Perhaps my acting career had come to an end. Who knew? But it had been full enough and colourful enough to have encouraged one newspaper to serialize my life story.

And I remembered that poem of Longfellow's from the Psalm of Life, memorized all those years ago when I was a wee girl in Kilmun Home recovering from Grannie's death,

> *Lives of great men all remind us*
> *We can make our lives sublime,*
> *And departing leave behind us,*
> *Footprints on the sands of time.*

Looking back on *The McFlannels*, on *Itma* and on *Life with the Lyons*, I hoped I could truthfully claim that I had left one small footprint.

Postscript

A week after I knew that this manuscript had been accepted, Barbara Lyon rang me to tell me the sad news that Ben had died of a heart attack in his first-class suite aboard the *QE 2*. Only the previous night, Barbara had joked with me on the telephone, 'Daddy is in Japan. He's working the boats.' This was her humorous way of describing his job as entertainment director of the liner, and of his performances as lecturer and raconteur. He entertained packed lounges with stories and anecdotes of the great early days of the movie industry, and he illustrated his talks with clips from Hollywood films and early TV shows. He was a professional to his finger-tips, and I heard from people who had attended his lectures, that he was a brilliant success.

Now Barbara was telling me he was dead. Of a heart attack. He had known nothing, and had suffered no pain. For this mercy we were grateful.

Having nursed Bebe for seven years, and having seen at first hand the tension and suffering a crippling illness imposes on the dignity of the human spirit, Ben would, I know, have chosen to go as he did. Still working, dying almost literally with his boots on. Nobody could ask for more, at the end of a long full life.

But it was bitter news all the same.

After the first lurching of the heart, with the shock of his death, I realized, with an added pang of anguish, that the secret I had kept from him that *One Small Footprint* was dedicated to him, would be hidden from him forever.

Oh, how I wished I had given him even the smallest hint. But I had wanted it to be a surprise.

I had planned that the first copy would wing its way to the States, as a small tribute to our long friendship. A friendship which had spilled over into our everyday lives from the working relationship in studio and on stage. I had gone into a day-dream of anticipation, trying to visualize his pleasure when he read the dedication, and realized how well I'd remembered his wise words to me.

But, as Rabbie truly says, 'The best-laid schemes of mice and men gang aft agley, an' leave us nought but grief an' pain for promised joy.'

Or could Barbara be right?

Maybe he does know.

I hope so. Oh, with all my heart, I hope so.

MOLLY WEIR